745.59412 ROD

8158

Glorious gifts.

9x 1/04 LT 1/03

7X 1/02 LT 1/02

Rodale's Treasury of Christmas Crafts

Glorious Gifts

Rodale's Treasury of Christmas Crafts

Glorious Gifts

Rodale Press, Emmaus, Pennsylvania

Our Mission
We publish books that empower people's lives.

RODALE BOOKS

Rodale Press Staff

Executive Editor
Margaret Lydic Balitas

Copy Editor
Carolyn R. Mandarano

Editor
Karen Bolesta

Book Designer
Patricia Field

If you have any questions or comments concerning this book, please write to:

Rodale Press, Inc.
Book Readers' Service
33 East Minor Street
Emmaus, PA 18098

Printed in the United States of America

Published by Rodale Press, Inc.
Distributed in the book trade by St. Martin's Press

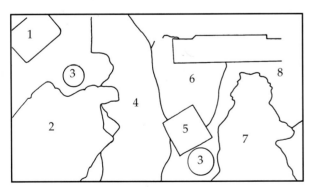

Projects on Cover: (1) Winter Wonder Postcard Box, (2) Be Pre"pear"ed Stenciled Apron, (3) Holiday Wreath Jar Lids, (4) The Biggest Knit Stocking of All, (5) Handmade Holiday Greetings, (6) Holly-Day Sweatshirt, (7) Christmas Plaid Bear and (8) Radish Garden Quilt

For Chapelle Ltd.

Owner
Jo Packham

Staff
Trice Boerens   Jackie McCowen
Gaylene Byers   Barbara Milburn
Holly Fuller   Pamela Randall
Cherie Hanson   Jennifer Roberts
Susan Jorgensen   Florence Stacey
Margaret Shields Marti Nancy Whitley

Photography
Ryne Hazen

Book Design, Project Design and Text
Chapelle Ltd., Ogden, Utah 84401 © 1993 by Chapelle Ltd.

The photographs in this book were taken at Mary Gaskill's Trends and Traditions, Ogden, Utah. Her trust and cooperation are deeply appreciated.

The author and editors who compiled this book have tried to make all of the contents as accurate and as correct as possible. Graphs, illustrations, photographs and text have all been carefully checked and cross-checked. However, due to the variability of local conditions, tools and supplies, personal skill and so on, Rodale Press assumes no responsibility for any injuries suffered or for damages or other losses incurred that result from the material presented herein. All instructions should be carefully studied and clearly understood before beginning a project.

Library of Congress Cataloging-in-Publication Data
Glorious gifts.
    p. cm. -- (Rodale's treasury of Christmas crafts)
    ISBN 0–87596–600–4 hardcover
    1. Christmas decorations. 2. Handicraft. I. Rodale Press.
II. Series.
TT900 . C4G53 1993
745 . 594 ' 12--dc20   93–22565
                                   CIP

2 4 6 8 10 9 7 5 3 1 hardcover

ontents

Be Pre"pear"ed Stenciled Apron

Golden ripe pears line up on this pretty apron, brightening the day for cook and kitchen.

MATERIALS

Purchased butcher's apron
7" x 8" sheet of Mylar
8" x 9" piece of mat board
Tape
Craft knife
Ruler
Dressmaker's pen
Acrylic paints: dark green, olive green,
   light green, brown, yellow,
   straw, antique gold, raw sienna
Acrylic texture medium
One small dish for each color of paint
Paintbrushes

DIRECTIONS

1. Trace pears and checks patterns on page 125 onto Mylar. Tape Mylar to mat board. Using craft knife, cut out areas to be stenciled. Cut stencils apart, leaving pears, leaves and stems as a unit to ensure accurate placement.

2. Mix paints with texture medium according to manufacturer's instructions.

3. Place apron on work surface. Stencil one row of checks along top edge of apron bib, using olive green paint; see photo. Allow to dry. Stencil second row below first, staggering checks for checkerboard effect. Repeat along bottom edge of apron, stenciling first row of checks along hem. Allow to dry.

4. Measure 2½" below second row of checks on apron bib; mark. Also mark vertical center of apron. Center and stencil first set of pear leaves with tops on 2½" mark, using olive green. Accent leaves with dark green and light green, working through stencil for crisp edges. Allow to dry. Stencil first set of pear stems in place, using brown paint. Allow to dry. Stencil first set of pears in place, using yellow paint. Shade pears with straw and raw sienna, working outward from center; highlight outer edges with antique gold. Repeat with sets of pears on either side of first set as needed to fill width of bib. Allow to dry.

5. Measure 5¼" above checks at apron hem, centering and stenciling first set of pear leaves with tops on 5¼" mark. Repeat remainder of Step 4, stenciling as many sets of pears as needed to fill width of apron; see photo. Allow all to dry.

6. When paint is completely dry, place cloth over apron and iron on low setting to set paint.

Holly~Day Sweatshirt

Christmas colors of red, green and gold combine with warm plaid for a buttoned-up and holiday-perfect sweatshirt.

MATERIALS

Purchased white sweatshirt
Tracing paper
Soft lead pencil
One 11" x 14" sheet of Mylar
Dressmaker's pen
Drafting tape
Scrap of mat board
Craft knife
Acrylic paints: green, metallic gold
Paintbrushes
¼ yard of plaid fabric; matching thread
Seven gold buttons
Fifty-two sew-on rhinestones

DIRECTIONS

1. Trace ribbon pattern on page 10 and holly leaves pattern on page 11. Transfer patterns to Mylar, leaving 2" margin around each. Draw ribbon and holly separately. Holly is stencil A; see diagram. Cut out stencils along margins. Tape to mat board. Using craft knife, cut out areas to be stenciled. To make stencil B, reverse holly pattern and repeat; see diagram.

2. Using dressmaker's pen, draw a vertical line down center front of shirt. Position ribbon in stencil A on left side of shirt front, 1½" below neckline and beginning 1½" left of centerline; see diagram. Stencil ribbon gold. End at

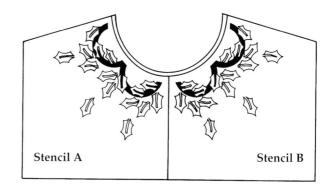

Stencil A   Stencil B

Diagram

shoulder seam. Repeat on right side of shirt, using same ribbon stencil. Allow to dry.

3. Place holly stencil A over ribbon stencil, beginning 1" left of centerline, and paint green. Repeat on right side of shirt, using holly stencil B. Allow to dry.

4. Cut shirt open along centerline. From plaid fabric, cut two 3" x (length of opening plus ½") strips to make plackets. Fold plackets in half lengthwise and press; turn under ¼" on one long edge and press. With right sides facing, pin long unpressed edge of one placket to one cut edge, so placket extends ¼" over top and bottom of sweatshirt. Sew ¼" seam along long edge. Fold strip back over itself so sewn edge and turned-under raw edge are even and right sides are facing. Sew a ¼" seam across upper and lower edges. Trim seams and clip corners. Turn placket. Slip-stitch in place along inside long edge. Repeat for second placket.

5. Allow right placket to overlap left placket. Make seven buttonholes evenly spaced apart on right placket, beginning ½" below neckline. Sew gold buttons opposite buttonholes on left placket.

6. Stitch rhinestones to stenciled area of shirt as desired; see photo.

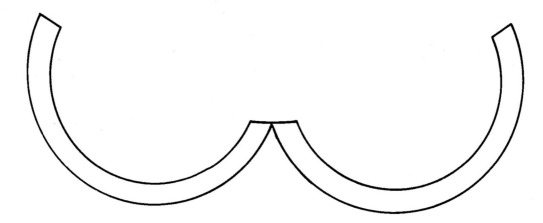

Ribbon Pattern

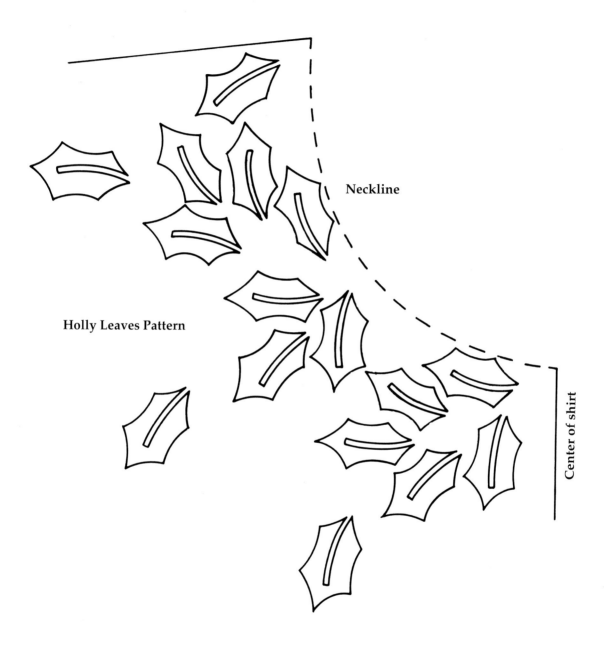

Neckline

Holly Leaves Pattern

Center of shirt

Christmas Plaid Bear

Create this adorable bear dressed in holiday finery! She'll watch happily over all your festive activities.

MATERIALS

½ yard of golden tan distressed mohair or other deep-pile fake fur; matching thread
Carpet thread and carpet needle (for basting, ladder stitching and attaching eyes)
Scrap of tan felt
18" x 18" piece of poster board
Tracing paper
Pencil
Single-edge razor blade
Moustache scissors
Awl
Four 2"-wide plastic snap-to doll joints
Polyester stuffing
Wooden spoon
Large-eyed needle
Black pearl cotton size 5
Two ⅜"-diameter plastic button eyes
⅜ yard of cranberry/black plaid corduroy; matching thread
2¾ yards of double-fold black bias tape; matching thread
One 10"-diameter doily
Two ½"-diameter buttons
One snap
Purchased hat for 18"-tall doll with black netting, ribbon bow and ties, dried berries, miniature dried flowers and tiny pinecones*
Hot glue gun and glue sticks
Hat pin

*See "Suppliers" on page 128.

DIRECTIONS

All seams are ¼". Sew all seams in direction of nap of fur.

1. Trace patterns for bear on pages 16, 17, 18, 19 and 20, transferring all information. Transfer to poster board. Outline each on wrong side of fur, noting direction of nap on pattern and flipping patterns as needed to get right- and left-facing pieces. When cutting patterns from fur, work from wrong side with single-edge razor, cutting through backing fabric only. Gently separate cut pieces from surrounding fur. Cut patterns as follows: Two right-facing legs; two left-facing legs; two outer arms; two inner arms; one head inset; one right-facing head; one left-facing head; four ears; one right-facing back; one left-facing back; one right-facing tummy; one left-facing tummy. From felt, cut two feet, one right-facing paw and one left-facing paw. Using awl, punch holes for joints through both backs according to pattern. Punch hole for joint through one right-facing leg and one left-facing leg according to pattern; these will become the inner legs. Punch hole for joint through both inner arms according to pattern.

2. Note: Before machine-sewing pieces together, baste seams, then turn to check fit and curves. Turn back to wrong side and brush fur away from seams. Machine-sew seams; remove basting. After sewing, use a straight pin to pull fur from seams.

3. With right sides facing, sew one inner and outer leg together, leaving openings at bottom and top according to pattern. With right sides facing, baste one felt foot in bottom opening; sew. Remove basting. Turn. Slide Disk A onto shank section of doll joint; see Diagram 1. Insert doll joint through hole in wrong side of inner leg so shank protrudes through right side of fur. Stuff leg, using wooden spoon to tamp stuffing down as needed. Ladder-stitch opening closed; see Diagram 2. Repeat with remaining inner and outer legs and one doll joint. Set aside.

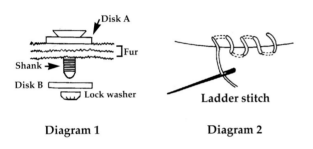

Diagram 1   Diagram 2

4. With right sides facing, sew straight edge of one felt paw to one inner arm according to pattern. Repeat with remaining paw and inner arm. With right sides facing, stitch outer arm to inner arm, leaving opening at top according to pattern. Slide Disk A onto shank section of doll joint as in Step 2. Insert doll joint through hole in inner arm so shank protrudes through right side of fur. Repeat remainder of Step 2. Repeat with remaining paw and arms and one doll joint.

5. Sew dart on left- and right-facing bear heads according to pattern. With right sides facing, sew the head pieces together along the center front seam from the tip of the nose (large dot) to the neck. With right sides facing and starting at dot, pin head inset to head, matching large dots and leaving opening at bottom according to pattern. Beginning at dot, baste, then sew seam, easing in any fullness in facial area. Sew gathering threads around neck opening; do not cut thread. Turn.

6. Stuff muzzle firmly. Determine desired position of eyes and mark. Using carpet thread and needle, sew button eyes to front of head as follows. Begin sewing inside head front, bringing needle out at one eye placement. Thread one button eye onto needle and return needle through eye placement to inside of head front. Sew through eye placement and button eye several times, pulling thread tightly to indent eye. Bring needle down through same button eye, then across muzzle inside head front and out at other eye placement. Thread remaining button eye onto needle, pulling thread tightly between eyes. Repeat sewing as for first eye. Knot thread. Fluff fur around each eye. Stuff head firmly.

7. Slide Disk A onto shank section of doll joint as in Step 2. Insert doll joint into neck opening, with shank protruding from center of opening. Tighten gathering threads around shank; secure.

8. With right sides facing, sew two ears together, leaving bottom open. Turn. Stuff. Ladder-stitch opening closed. Repeat with remaining ears. Pin ears to head in desired position; sew in place. Using moustache scissors, trim mohair to ⅛" length on muzzle, following lines on head and head inset patterns. When trimming close to lines, begin tapering fur back to original length. Using black floss and large-eyed needle, satin-stitch nose. Embroider mouth in desired expression; see Diagram 3.

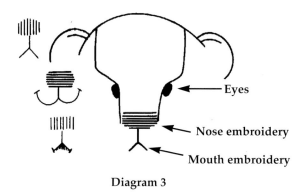

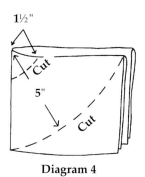

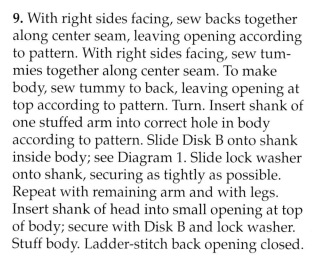

Diagram 3

Eyes

Nose embroidery

Mouth embroidery

Diagram 4

1½"

Cut

5"

Cut

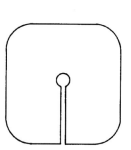

Diagram 5

9. With right sides facing, sew backs together along center seam, leaving opening according to pattern. With right sides facing, sew tummies together along center seam. To make body, sew tummy to back, leaving opening at top according to pattern. Turn. Insert shank of one stuffed arm into correct hole in body according to pattern. Slide Disk B onto shank inside body; see Diagram 1. Slide lock washer onto shank, securing as tightly as possible. Repeat with remaining arm and with legs. Insert shank of head into small opening at top of body; secure with Disk B and lock washer. Stuff body. Ladder-stitch back opening closed.

10. To make cape, cut a 10" x 10" square from plaid fabric. To find center, fold fabric in fourths. Mark center on wrong side of fabric. Measure 1½" and 5" from center and mark curved lines; see Diagram 4. Cut fabric along curves; see Diagram 4. Unfold fabric. Cut along vertical centerline from outside long edge of fabric to cut-out center; see Diagram 5. Cut a 52" length of bias tape. Sew bias tape along edges of cape on right side, mitering corners; see "General Instructions" on page 126. Trim excess and turn ends under. Fold bias to wrong side of cape; slipstitch.

11. To make lace collar, fold doily in half. Cut in half along fold. Unfold one doily half and

center on right side of cape over neck opening. Fold doily 1" to wrong side of neck opening and front opening of cape; tack. Wrap cape around bear neck. Overlap edges of cape slightly at front. Secure by sewing on two buttons through all fabric layers; see photo.

12. For waistband, cut one 2½"-wide strip from plaid, long enough to fit around bear waist plus 1½" for overlap and seam allowances. Turn under ¼" on one long edge and press; set aside. For skirt, cut a 27" x 8½" piece from plaid. With right sides facing, sew short ends of skirt together, leaving 1" at top unstitched; press seam open. Turn to right side. Sew gathering thread along top edge; do not cut thread. Gather skirt to fit bear's waist and secure thread. With right sides facing and leaving ¾" of waistband free at each end, pin

15

unpressed long edge of waistband to gathered edge of skirt; sew in place. Fold strip back over itself so that sewn edge and turned-under raw edge are even and right sides are facing; sew across short edges using ¼" seam allowance. Trim seams and clip corners to eliminate bulk. Turn waistband to right side; slipstitch in place along inside long edge. Sew snap in place on waistband overlap.

13. Position hat on bear head. Secure with hat pin and ribbon ties.

— *Try This* —

Eye placement is important to your bear's expression. Large eyes set low and close together will create a cute, sweet-appearing bear. Small eyes set high and far apart create a wiser, older, more serious bear.

The embroidery of the mouth also affects expression. Diagram 3 shows several ways of embroidering the mouth. If your first attempt is not satisfactory, simply pull out the threads and restitch!

Last, ear placement also affects your bear's expression. Pin the ears in different places before deciding where to sew them.

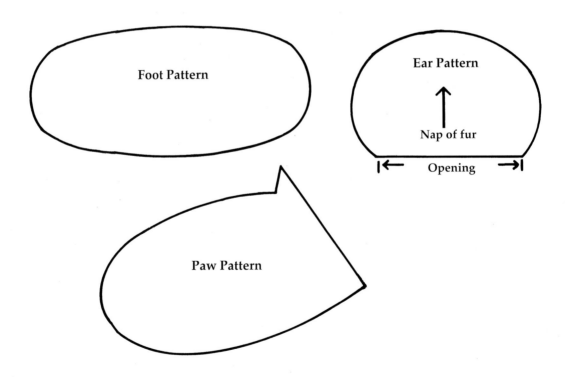

Foot Pattern

Ear Pattern

Nap of fur

|← Opening →|

Paw Pattern

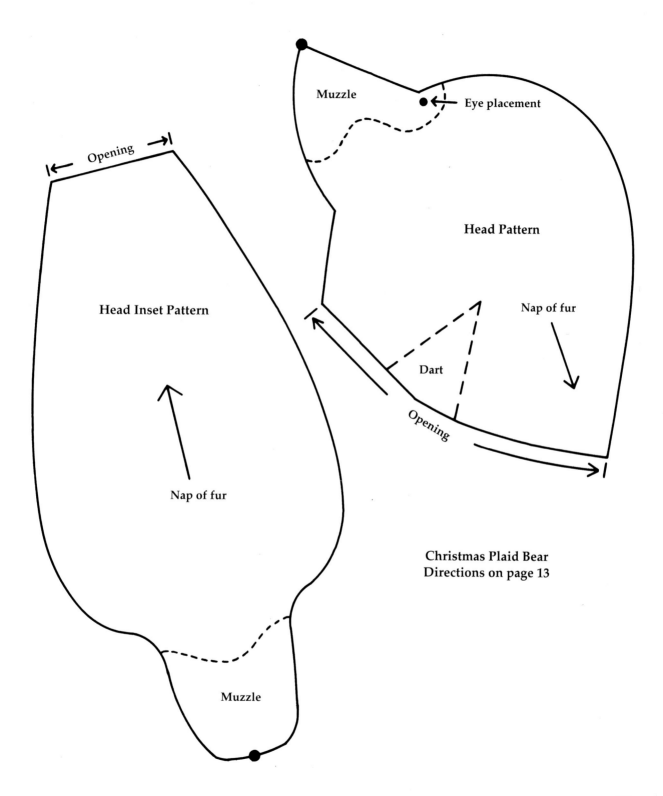

Muzzle

Eye placement

Head Pattern

Opening

Nap of fur

Head Inset Pattern

Dart

Nap of fur

Opening

Christmas Plaid Bear
Directions on page 13

Muzzle

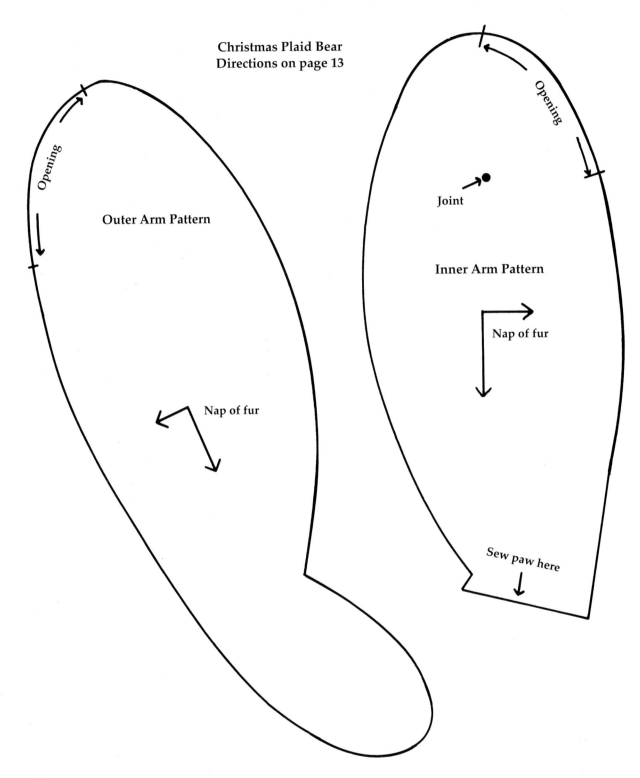

Christmas Plaid Bear
Directions on page 13

Opening

Outer Arm Pattern

Nap of fur

Opening

Joint

Inner Arm Pattern

Nap of fur

Sew paw here

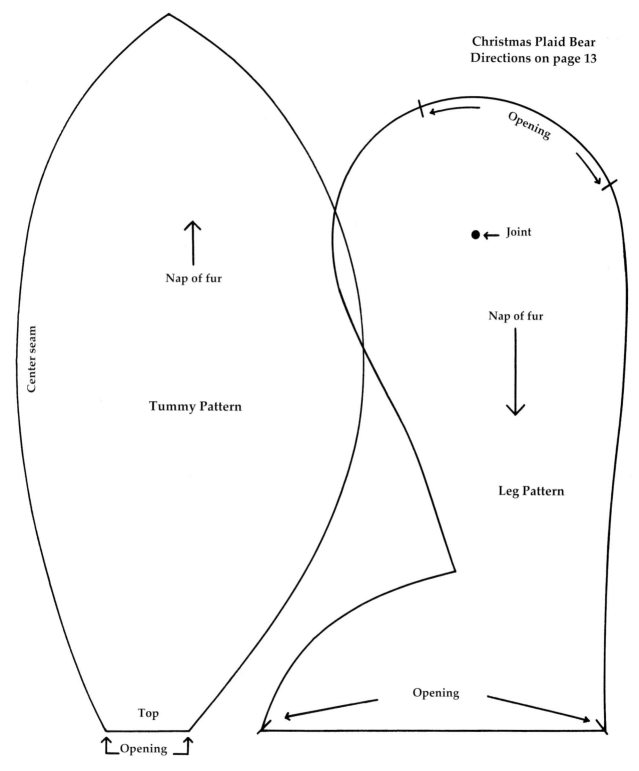

Christmas Plaid Bear
Directions on page 13

Opening

● ← Joint

Nap of fur

Center seam

Tummy Pattern

Nap of fur

Leg Pattern

Top

Opening

Opening

19

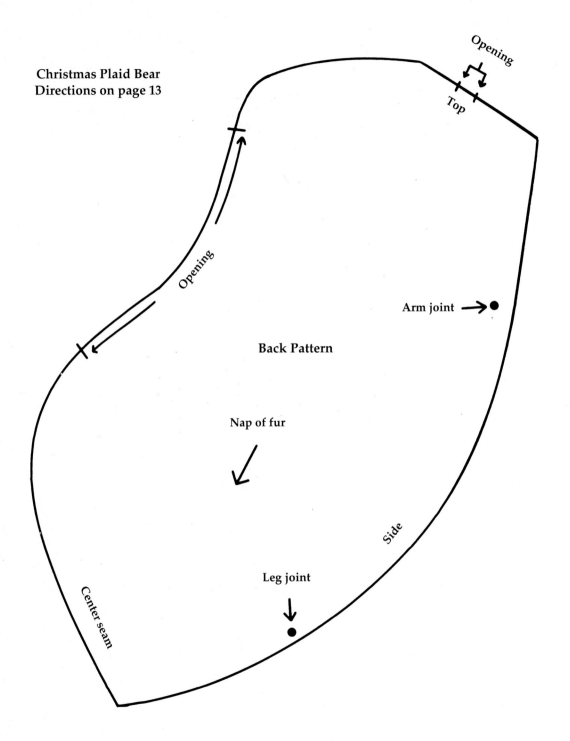

Christmas Plaid Bear
Directions on page 13

Opening

Top

Opening

Arm joint ●

Back Pattern

Nap of fur

Side

Center seam

Leg joint
↓
●

Opposite: Holiday Wreath Jar Lids

Holiday Wreath Jar Lids

Rather than choose between the delicate floral wreath and the classic evergreen wreath motif, just stitch both! (Projects pictured on previous page.)

MODEL (floral wreath)

Stitched on cream Aida 18 over one thread, the finished design size is 2" x 2". The fabric was cut 6" x 6". Insert completed design piece in porcelain jar lid* according to manufacturer's instructions.

*See "Suppliers" on page 128.

FABRICS	DESIGN SIZES
Aida 11	3⅜" x 3⅜"
Aida 14	2⅝" x 2⅝"
Hardanger 22	1⅝" x 1⅝"

MODEL (evergreen wreath)

Stitched on cream Aida 18 over one thread, the finished design size is 2" x 2". The fabric was cut 6" x 6". Insert completed design piece in porcelain jar lid* according to manufacturer's instructions.

*See "Suppliers" on page 128.

FABRICS	DESIGN SIZES
Aida 11	3¼" x 3¼"
Aida 14	2⅝" x 2⅝"
Hardanger 22	1⅝" x 1⅝"

Floral Wreath

DMC		Marlitt (used for sample)

Step 1: Cross-stitch (2 strands)

DMC	symbol	Marlitt	color
745	·	1013	Yellow
722	∴	807	Orange-lt.
3340	●	1044	Orange-med.
754	○	1042	Peach-lt.
3326	▲	830	Pink
335	✕	881	Rose
552	■	858	Purple
989	ı	897	Green-med.
319	╱	852	Green-dk.

Step 2: Backstitch (1 strand)

DMC	symbol	Marlitt	color
319	⌐	852	Green-dk.

Evergreen Wreath

DMC		Marlitt (used for sample)

Step 1: Cross-stitch (2 strands)

DMC	symbol	Marlitt	color
335	▲	881	Rose
3348	ı	1058	Green-lt.
989	∴	897	Green-med.
319	✕	852	Green-dk.
922	○	864	Tan

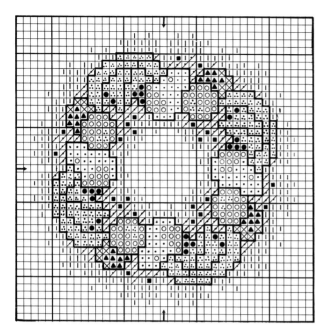

Floral Wreath
Stitch Count: 37 x 37

Holiday Wreath Jar Lids Graphs
Directions on page 22

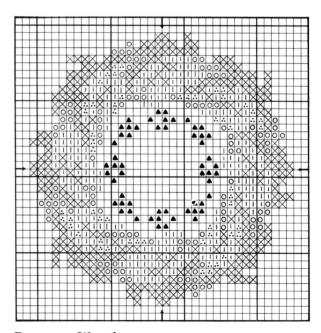

Evergreen Wreath
Stitch Count: 36 x 36

Mrs. Hippity-Hop

Pieced and quilted with love, this fashionable bunny is a welcome companion!

MATERIALS

Scraps of eight assorted print fabrics
Polyester stuffing
½ yard of flannel
Scraps of green/white striped fabric
Dressmaker's pen
Tracing paper
White thread
Two black 3mm beads
1 yard of ¼"-wide lilac ribbon
One miniature green straw hat
   with 2¼"-diameter brim

DIRECTIONS

All seams are ¼".

1. From print fabrics, cut 132 blocks, 2" x 2", reserving one 4" x 4" piece for bunny tail. With right sides facing, piece blocks into one twelve-block by eleven-block rectangle. From flannel, cut one matching rectangle. Baste to wrong side of pieced rectangle, aligning edges. Mark intersecting diagonal lines on pieced rectangle. Hand-quilt along lines with white thread.

2. Trace bunny patterns on pages 26 and 27; arrows on patterns indicate grain of fabric. From quilted rectangle, cut two bodies, two heads, two ears, four legs, one 16½" x 2¼" body inset and one 7" x 1½" bias strip for head inset. Cut one tail from 4" x 4" piece of print fabric. Cut two ears from green/white fabric.

3. With right sides facing, sew one head to one edge of head inset, leaving straight edge free. Sew remaining head along opposite edge of inset, matching placement of first head; leave straight edge open. Turn. Stuff firmly. Slipstitch opening closed; set aside.

4. With right sides facing, sew one body to body inset. Sew remaining body along opposite edge of inset, matching placement of first body and leaving an opening. Turn. To make feet in center front of inset, sew a 1" line through all layers of fabric, sewing toward head. Back tack. Stuff body firmly. Slipstitch opening closed; set aside.

5. With right sides facing, sew two legs together, leaving an opening. Turn. Stuff firmly. Repeat with remaining two legs. Place body, belly side down, on flat surface; see photo. Position one leg near back of body with bottom of leg resting on flat surface. Tack leg to body, keeping leg seam centered. Repeat with second leg, matching placement of first leg.

6. Slipstitch head securely to center of body inset 1½" above stitched line of feet; see photo.

7. With right sides facing, sew one quilted ear to one green/white ear, leaving an opening. Clip curves and turn. Slipstitch opening closed. Repeat with remaining quilted and green/white ears. Make a tuck in bottom of each ear; secure thread. Slipstitch one ear to each side of head; see photo for placement.

8. Sew a gathering thread around edge of tail. Do not cut thread. Gather loosely; stuff. Tighten thread and secure. Tack tail to center back of body inset; see photo for placement.

9. To make eyes, sew one black bead to each side of head. From lilac ribbon, cut two 9½" lengths. Glue one end of each to inside of hat at base of crown. From remaining lilac ribbon, cut two 8½" lengths. Handling as one, twist lengths loosely together and tie around hat for hat band. Notch ribbon tails. Place hat on bunny and tie "chin strap" tails in a bow. Trim ribbon tails to desired length and notch ends.

Try This

Plan a Mrs. Hippity-Hop birthday party for a child! Make one bunny for each small guest, saving time by using prequilted fabrics. Have lots of ribbons, miniature hats and other bunny beauty aids on hand to help the children dress and decorate their very own bunnies.

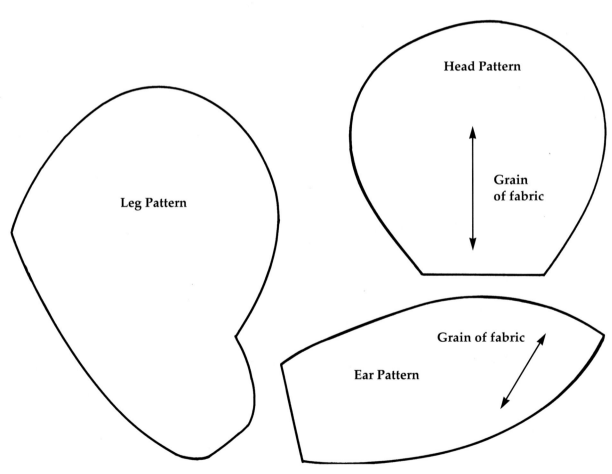

Leg Pattern

Head Pattern

Grain of fabric

Grain of fabric

Ear Pattern

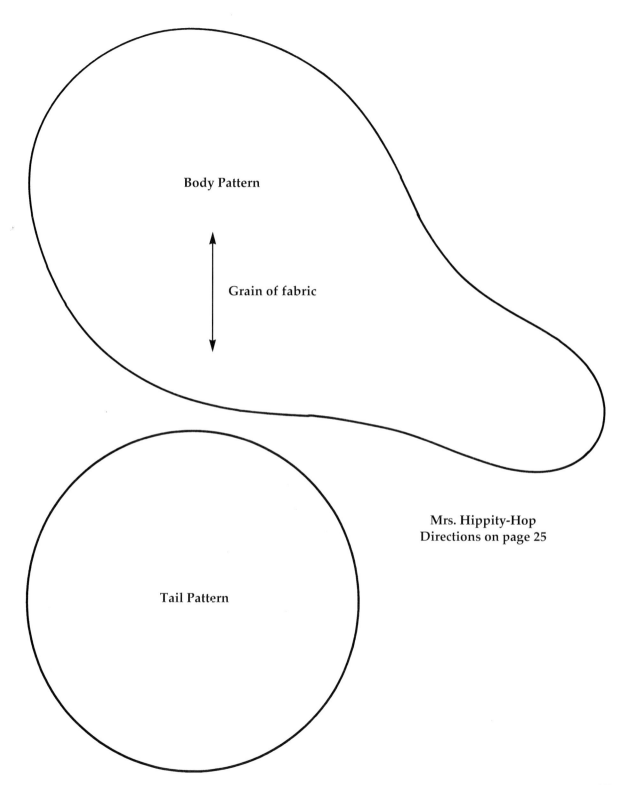

Body Pattern

Grain of fabric

Tail Pattern

Mrs. Hippity-Hop
Directions on page 25

27

Crispy Cabbage Pincushion

A little bit of the garden comes to the sewing table with this cabbage pincushion. You can make it in minutes! (Project pictured on page 24.)

MATERIALS

One 7¾"-diameter muslin circle
One 8¼"-diameter print fabric circle; matching thread
One 8¼"-diameter flannel circle
One 8¼"-diameter fleece circle
Five 6¼"-diameter green polished cotton circles; matching thread
Sawdust

DIRECTIONS

1. To make muslin inner bag, make a yo-yo by folding muslin circle's edges under ¼" and sewing a gathering thread ⅛" from fold; see diagram. Do not cut thread. Gather to make a 2"-diameter opening. Stuff firmly with sawdust. Tighten thread and secure. Shape bag so gathering is at center on top.

Diagram

2. To make cabbage head, layer flannel, fleece, then print fabric right side up; baste edges. Hand-quilt around motifs on print fabric. Remove basting. Make a yo-yo as in Step 1. Do not gather or cut thread. Center quilt sandwich over muslin bag. Tighten gathering thread around muslin bag and secure. Shape cabbage so layered gathering is at center on the bottom.

3. To make a cabbage leaf, make a yo-yo with one green circle. Flatten circle so gathering is at center. Repeat with remaining green circles.

4. Place leaves flat with gathered sides up and overlap edges to make a 7"-diameter circle. Slipstitch together, overlapping edges. Position cabbage head gathered side down in center of leaf circle; pin in place. Slipstitch bottom edges of leaves to bottom of cabbage head. Fold one leaf up; pinch center. Tack to cabbage head so leaf is slightly puckered; see photo. Repeat with remaining leaves.

Opposite: Appliquéd Wreath Stocking

Appliquéd Wreath Stocking

This bright red stocking will fill a room with Christmas cheer! (Project pictured on previous page.)

MATERIALS

¼ yard of red felt
6" x 6" piece of green felt; matching thread
Scrap of navy print fabric
⅝ yard of yellow print fabric
⅜ yard of red print fabric
Scrap of white felt; matching thread
Scrap of red-striped fabric
½ yard of paper-backed fusible webbing
¼ yard of fusible tear-away
Tracing paper
⅜ yard of variegated red wired ribbon

DIRECTIONS

1. Enlarge stocking pattern on page 33; see "General Instructions" on page 126. From red felt, cut two stockings. From tear-away, cut one stocking. For stocking lining pattern, add 1¼" to top of stocking pattern to allow for faux cuff. From yellow print fabric, cut two lining pieces. From red print fabric, cut 2"-wide bias strips, piecing as needed to equal 1⅛ yards of binding; set aside.

2. Trace appliqué patterns on pages 31 and 32. Transfer to paper side of fusible webbing, leaving at least ½" between each and drawing five stars. Cut out, leaving space around each; do not remove paper. Fuse rough side of wreath to green felt. Fuse stars to white felt. Fuse zigzag border and toe border to wrong side of navy print fabric. Fuse toe cap to wrong side of yellow print fabric and bow and bow tails to wrong side of red-striped fabric. Cut out appliqués. Remove paper.

3. One layer at a time, fuse appliqués to right side of one red felt stocking piece; see photo. Place shiny side of tear-away against wrong side of appliquéd stocking piece. Iron. Using green and white thread as desired, finish edges of appliqués with machine satin-stitching. To remove tear-away, lift at one corner and carefully tear. To remove from appliqués, make a small scissor cut in portion of tear-away backing appliqués; lift and tear.

4. Mark line 1¼" below and parallel to top edge of both felt stocking pieces. With right sides facing, layer one stocking piece and one lining piece, matching top edge of lining to marked line. Sew ¼" from lining edge. Repeat with remaining stocking and lining pieces. Fold lining pieces to back side of stocking pieces. Layer stocking back, then front, matching edges. Trim stockings and appliqués as needed to make edges even. Pin together.

5. With right sides facing, sew binding to stocking front, using ½" seam and folding ends under at top edge. Fold binding to stocking back and slipstitch, covering stitching line.

6. For hanger, twist variegated red ribbon loosely and make a loop. Tack inside top of stocking back on heel side.

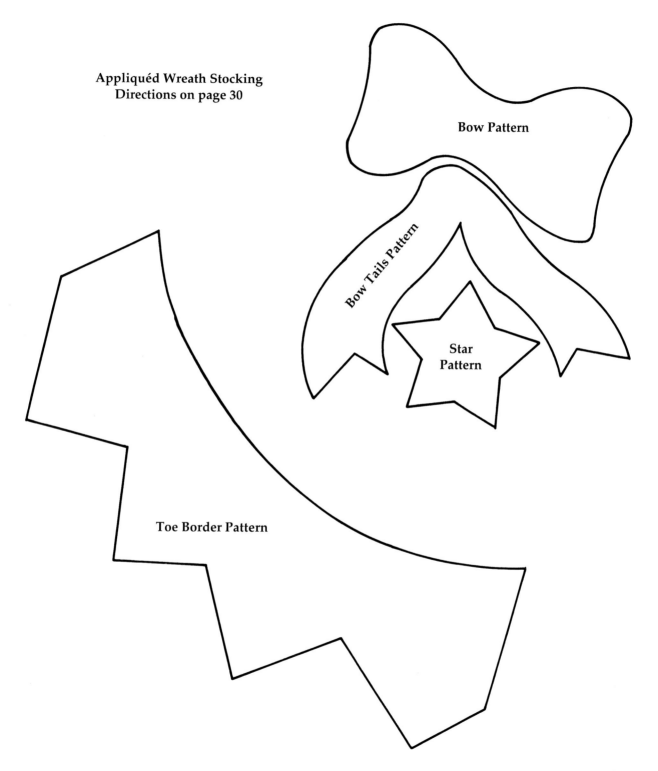

Appliquéd Wreath Stocking
Directions on page 30

Bow Pattern

Bow Tails Pattern

Star
Pattern

Toe Border Pattern

31

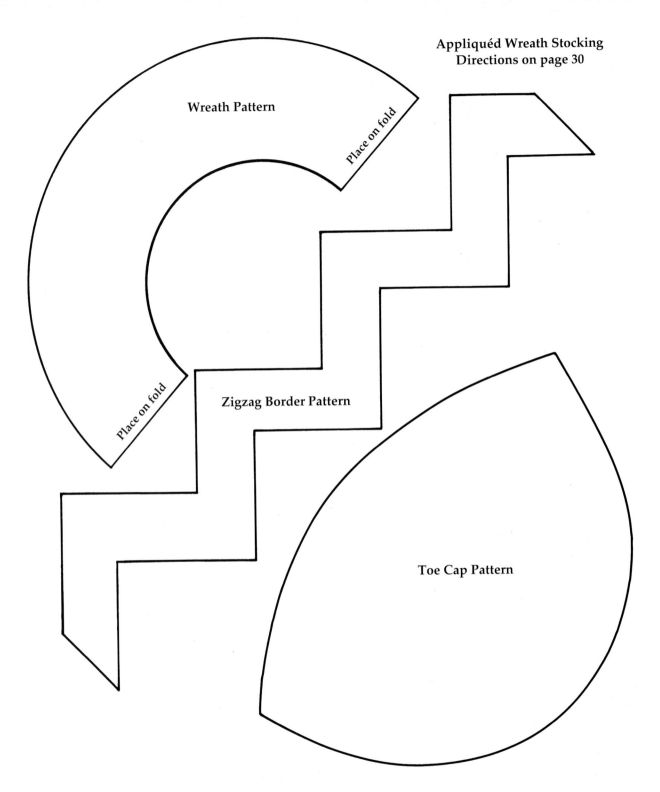

Appliquéd Wreath Stocking
Directions on page 30

Wreath Pattern

Place on fold

Place on fold

Zigzag Border Pattern

Toe Cap Pattern

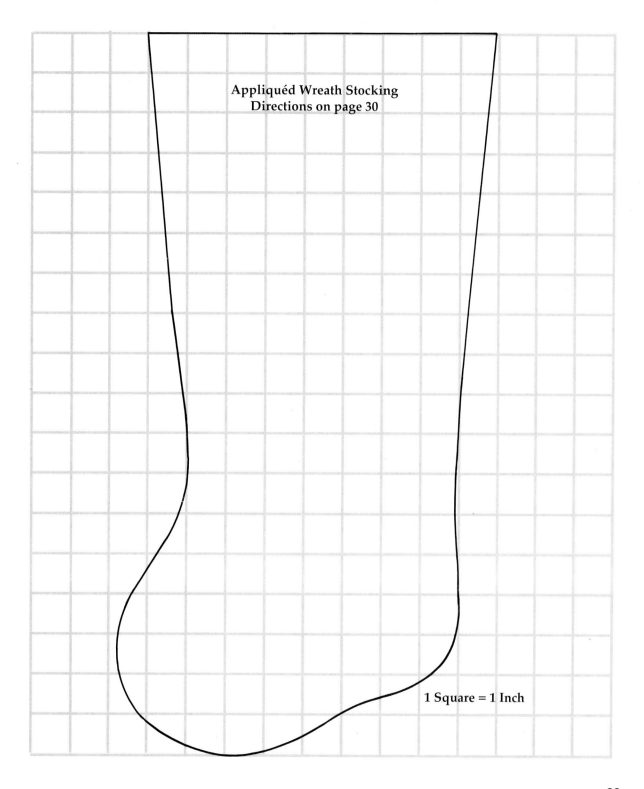

Appliquéd Wreath Stocking
Directions on page 30

1 Square = 1 Inch

Evergreen Flowerpot Carrier

The subtle colors of this old-fashioned carrier provide a dramatic setting for seasonal potted poinsettias.

MATERIALS

Purchased wooden carrier or crate
Three purchased wooden tree cutouts of
   desired size
Newspaper
Four unpainted clay flowerpots and saucers
Acrylic paints: red, dark green
Paintbrush
Cotton rag
Medium-grit sandpaper
Hot glue gun and glue sticks

DIRECTIONS

1. Place carrier or crate and tree cutouts on newspaper. Paint all sides red, allowing each side to dry before turning over. Paint two flowerpots and saucers red, remaining pots and saucers green. Allow to dry.

2. Dilute green paint with water to the consistency of ink. Dip cotton rag in paint; squeeze until wet but not dripping. Wipe green paint over red paint on carrier and trees. Allow to dry.

3. To achieve antique effect, sand edges of carrier and trees to expose red paint; see photo.

4. Glue trees to handle of carrier; see photo. If using a crate, glue trees along one top edge. Place plants in pots as desired and arrange in carrier.

Try This

For an added touch of warmth, display favorite Christmas cards among the pots, or surround the pots with glitter-dusted evergreen boughs.

Handmade Holiday Greetings

A handmade card says "I care." Though these are inexpensive to make, they'll add a priceless personal touch to someone's holidays.

MATERIALS (for Christmas tree card)

6" x 12" piece of bristol board
8" x 8" piece of rose stationery
¼ yard of green velveteen
¼ yard of paper-backed fusible webbing
Tracing paper
Dressmaker's pen
½ yard of ½"-wide gathered lace trim
¼ yard of 1¼"-wide gathered lace trim
Hot glue gun and glue sticks

¾ yard of ⅜"-wide rose ribbon
Permanent spray adhesive
½ yard of ⅛"-wide dusty rose silk ribbon
½ yard of ⅛"-wide deep rose silk ribbon
¼ yard of 1"-wide burgundy ribbon
½ yard of ⅛"-wide gold cord
Two brass charms
Six assorted faux pearls and shiny buttons
½ yard of ⅛"-wide green cord

DIRECTIONS

1. Trace Christmas tree pattern on page 39. From bristol board, cut one tree according to pattern for backing and one tree ⅛" smaller. From stationery, cut one tree according to larger pattern; set aside. Transfer one tree to paper side of fusible webbing. Cut out ½" outside tree outline. Fuse rough side of webbing tree to wrong side of green velveteen. Cut out tree. Remove paper.

2. Position velveteen tree on backing, aligning edges. Fuse. Starting at tree trunk, hot-glue ½"-wide trim along edges of backing so that ¼" of trim shows from velveteen side of tree, overlapping ends slightly. Trim excess. Repeat to glue 1¼"-wide trim along base of tree against wrong side of ½"-wide trim, allowing ¾" to show from velveteen side.

3. To make fluted edge, glue end of rose ribbon to backing, beginning slightly above lowest branch of tree. Loop so that ½" of ribbon shows from velveteen side of tree; glue. Repeat, making a series of even loops along tree edge, ending slightly above lowest branch of tree on opposite side; see diagram. Glue one end of gold cord to backing, near treetop. Cascade cord as desired across velveteen side of tree, securing with glue. Glue opposite end to backing near tree bottom.

4. To make a ribbon rosette, cut one 7" length each from dusty rose and deep rose silk ribbons. Repeat Step 2F for "Keepsake Heart Brooch" on page 42. Glue rosettes to

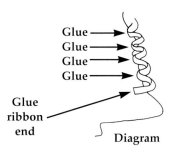

Glue →
Glue →
Glue →
Glue →
Glue ribbon end →

Diagram

velveteen side of tree as desired. Handling as one, knot remaining dusty rose and deep rose ribbon at 1¼" intervals. To make a cascading ribbon border, glue one end of knotted ribbon to lower left corner of backing. Drape ribbon around tree front near bottom and right-hand edges, gluing knots to tree; see photo. Glue opposite end of ribbon to backing near tree-top.

5. Coat one side of remaining bristol board tree with spray adhesive. Glue to backing, aligning edges. Allow glue to set. Coat one side of stationery tree with spray adhesive. Center and glue to bristol board side of velveteen tree. Allow glue to set.

6. From burgundy ribbon, cut one 6" length and one 1" length. Loop 6" length, slightly overlapping short ends in center of loop. Glue ends together. Flatten loop into bow. Wrap 1" ribbon around bow center. Glue ends together under bow. With ends underneath, glue bow to center of tree base on velveteen side.

7. Hot-glue faux pearls, buttons and charms to velveteen tree as desired. Knot ends of green cord. Glue center of cord to stationery side of tree ¾" from treetop.

MATERIALS (for angel card)

One 8½" x 11" sheet of patterned stationery
One 8½" x 11" sheet of plain stationery
¼ yard of cream fabric with metallic accents
6" x 6" piece of lace
¼ yard of paper-backed fusible webbing
Tracing paper
Dressmaker's pen
Permanent spray adhesive
⅝ yard of flat gold braid
⅝ yard of ¹⁄₁₆"-wide gold cord
⅜ yard of ⅛"-wide beige silk ribbon
⅜ yard of ⅛"-wide cream silk ribbon
⅜ yard of ⅛"-wide tan silk ribbon
⅜ yard of ⅛"-wide taupe silk ribbon
⅜ yard of ⅛"-wide off-white silk ribbon
One cream button

DIRECTIONS

1. From patterned stationery, cut one 9" x 4¾" piece. From plain stationery, cut one 8½" x 4½" piece. From lace, cut one 4½" x 4¾" piece. Match short edges of patterned stationery to find center. Carefully fold along center. Trim edges as needed so they match. Open folded card and place patterned side up on work surface. Cover left half of card with piece of scrap paper. Coat right half with spray adhesive. Smooth lace over coated area of stationery. Allow glue to set. Trim edges of lace to match card edges.

2. Trace angel pattern on page 39. Transfer to paper side of fusible webbing. Cut out ½" outside angel outline. Fuse rough side of webbing angel to wrong side of fabric. Cut out angel. Remove paper. Center angel on lace. Fuse. Beginning at underarm, hot-glue gold cord around edges of angel. Hot-glue gold braid along edges of lace. Place angel card decorated side down on clean work surface.

3. Match short edges of plain stationery to find center. Carefully fold along center. Trim edges as needed so they match. Coat undeco-rated side of angel card with spray adhesive. Center plain stationery on angel card, match-ing folds. Smooth plain stationery in place.

4. Handling the five ⅛"-wide ribbon lengths as one, tie in bow. Trim ends to desired length; knot. Hot-glue bow to angel's waist. Hot-glue button to center of bow.

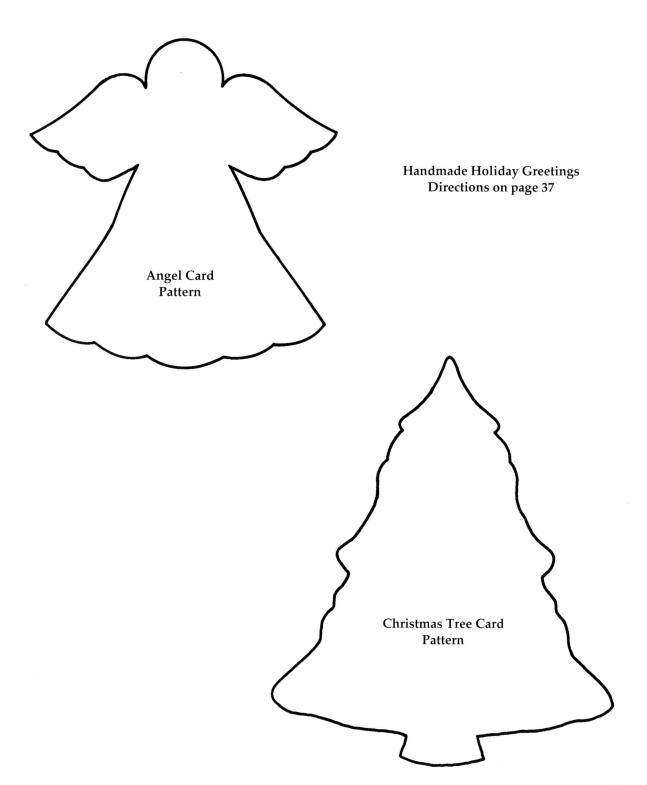

Angel Card
Pattern

Handmade Holiday Greetings
Directions on page 37

Christmas Tree Card
Pattern

39

eepsake Heart Brooch

Ribbon rosebuds and gentle colors combine to create a charming brooch with Victorian flair.

MATERIALS

6" x 6" scrap of mat board
Scrap of pale lilac fabric
Scrap of fleece
Tracing paper
Dressmaker's pen
Craft knife
¾ yard of ⅛"-wide dusty rose silk ribbon
⅜ yard of ⅛"-wide beige silk ribbon
⅜ yard of ⅛"-wide coral silk ribbon
⅜ yard of ⅛"-wide pale gray silk ribbon
⅜ yard of ⅛"-wide deep rose silk ribbon
Embroidery floss: dusty rose, deep rose, lilac, pale green

Large-eyed needle
Assorted metallic seed beads and small faux pearls
Hot glue gun and glue sticks
Tacky glue
Small glue brush
¼ yard of ½"-wide crocheted or tatted trim
Purchased ¾"-long pin back
⅛ yard of ¾"-wide taupe ribbon
¼ yard of 1"-wide rose ribbon
¼ yard of ⅛"-wide gold cord

DIRECTIONS

1. Trace heart pattern on page 42. Using craft knife, cut two hearts from mat board. On lilac fabric, outline two hearts for brooch back and front, adding ½" seam allowance; do not cut out. From fleece, cut one heart.

2. This step contains specifics for decorating brooch front; see Embellishment Diagram and Color Key on page 42 for stitch, bead, faux pearl and color placement. Leave brooch front seam allowance and brooch back unstitched.

A. To make a bullion stitch petal, see Diagrams 1A–1D. Using one strand of floss and keeping floss loose, bring needle up at 1 and down at 2. Bring needle tip out again at 1, but do not pull needle completely through fabric. Wrap floss around needle tip thirteen times. Holding finger over wrapped area, pull needle through floss. Insert needle again at 2, pulling to fabric back. If desired, pull floss slightly to curve bullion petal.

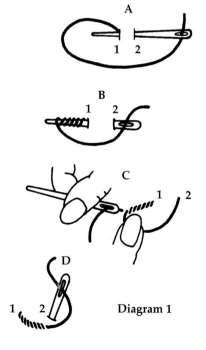

Diagram 1

B. To make a ribbon petal, see Diagram 2. Bring needle up at 1, then down at 2, slightly arcing ribbon.

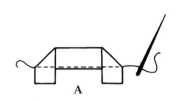

A

Diagram 2

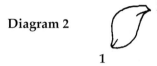

C. To make a leaf, see Diagram 3. Use two strands of floss.

Diagram 3

B

C

Diagram 5

D. To make a ribbon border, cut a 6" length of dusty rose ribbon. Bring needle up at 1, down at 2 and back up at a new 1; see Diagram 4. Twist ribbon loosely for ruffled effect. Secure ribbon end on wrong side of fabric; trim excess.

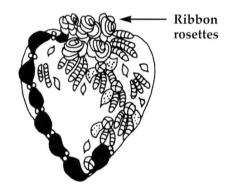

Ribbon rosettes

E. Sew beads and faux pearls to brooch as indicated.

Diagram 4

F. To make ribbon rosettes, cut a 9" length of each color of 1/8"-wide ribbon as indicated on Color Key. For one rosette, fold ribbon ends at right angles; this helps begin and end rosette. For a crisper rose, press ribbon. Sew a running thread along one long edge, leaving needle and thread attached; see Diagram 5A. Slightly gather ribbon, simultaneously wrapping ribbon to make rosette; see Diagram 5B. Force needle through lower ribbon edge to secure rosette in place as it is formed. When 1½" of ribbon remains, begin shaping ruffled base by looping and tacking folds of ribbon at underside of rosette; see Diagram 5C. Make

Embellishment Diagram

- = Ribbon border
- = Bullion stitch petal
- ○ = Bead
- ⊗ = Faux pearl
- ◇ = Leaf
- ◉ = Ribbon petal

Color Key
Ribbon rosettes = Dusty rose, coral, beige, deep rose, pale gray
Ribbon border = Dusty rose
Bullion stitch petals = Dusty rose, deep rose, lilac
Leaves = Pale green
Ribbon petals = Dusty rose

one rosette of each color. Sew rosettes to brooch front as indicated on the Embellishment Diagram.

3. Cut out brooch front and back along seam allowance.

4. To assemble brooch, place one mat board heart on work surface. Apply small amount of tacky glue to heart. Smooth fleece heart onto glued mat board, aligning edges. Allow to dry.

5. Place brooch front right side down on work surface. Center mat board heart fleece side down on brooch front and apply small amount of tacky glue to back of mat board. Fold brooch front seam allowance to back of mat board, keeping even tension and clipping curves as necessary. Check brooch front for smoothness. If no adjustment is needed, apply additional glue to secure fabric.

6. To finish brooch back, apply thin coat of tacky glue to one surface of remaining mat board heart. Center remaining fabric heart right side up over mat board heart. Smooth fabric onto mat board. Allow to dry. Fold seam allowance to back, keeping even tension and clipping curves as needed for smooth fit. Secure with tacky glue.

7. Glue crocheted trim along edges of wrong side of brooch front, allowing ¼" of trim to

Heart Pattern
Add ½"
seam allowance

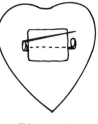

Diagram 6

show from right side. Glue brooch front to back, matching edges. Hot-glue pin back to center of brooch back ½" below top of heart. Cut one 1½" length of taupe ribbon. Loop ribbon so that short ends meet in center. With ends underneath, hot-glue loop over center of pin back base; see Diagram 6.

8. Cut one 6½" length of gold cord. Using tacky glue, attach cord along brooch edge between crochet trim and brooch back, beginning and ending at top of heart. Trim excess. From 1"-wide rose ribbon, cut one 5" length and one 1" length. Loop 5" length so that short ends overlap slightly in center of loop. Glue ends together. Flatten loop into bow. Wrap 1" length around bow center. Glue ends together under bow. With ends underneath, hot-glue bow to top center of heart back. Bead glue at bottom of bow center and under bottom edge of bow on each side, allowing only top of bow to show from front.

--- *Try This* ---

Glue the Keepsake Heart to a place card for the guest of honor at a holiday table.

To make a lovely miniature wreath, wrap a small grapevine wreath with coordinating ribbons and glue several hearts to the wreath.

Keepsake Hearts would also make delightful additions to the lid of the fabric "Keepsake Box" on page 44. Make the hearts in colors that match the fabric chosen for the box and hot-glue one on each corner of the lid.

eepsake Box

Present this pretty jewelry box just as it is or tuck a second gift inside—either way you'll earn compliments!

MATERIALS

Three 14" x 15" sheets of mat board
One 9" x 5" piece of lightweight cardboard
Ruler
T-square or carpenter's square
Triangle
Pencil
Utility knife
Scissors or rotary cutter
Masking tape
Dressmaker's pen
¾ yard of 44"-wide fabric
Thin-bodied tacky glue
Glue brush or roller

DIRECTIONS

1. Use a T-square and triangle to assure accurate right angles when measuring and marking mat board and cardboard. From mat board, cut one 14⁵⁄₁₆" x 12⁷⁄₁₆" piece for box, four 7" x 9" pieces and two 3" x 9" pieces for box jacket and one 9⁷⁄₁₆" x 7" piece for tray. From cardboard, cut one 8¾" x 3¹⁵⁄₁₆" piece for divider.

2. From fabric, cut one 23³⁄₁₆" x 3½" piece for box covering, one 15⁵⁄₁₆" x 13⁷⁄₁₆" piece for box lining, one 19" x 11" piece for box jacket covering, one 8½" x 8" piece for box jacket lining, one 8" x 10½" piece for tray lining, one 2½" x 22" piece for tray covering, one 3¾" x 6" piece for tray underside and one 10" x 5" piece for divider covering.

3. Score box piece; see Diagram 1. Do not fold. Place box scored side down on work surface. Coat with glue. Make sure fingers are free of glue before handling fabric. With fabric right side up, center box lining over box. Smooth onto glued surface. Trim fabric flush with cut-out corners only; see Diagram 2. Fold remaining excess fabric to other side of mat board; glue. Allow glue to set for 5 minutes. With fabric inside, carefully fold box along scored lines. Using masking tape inside of box, affix corners temporarily, checking to make sure they are straight and square.

4. Except for one long side and box bottom, coat outside of box with glue up to but not over top edges. Make sure fingers are free of glue before handling fabric. Smooth box covering onto outside of box, allowing ¼" of fabric to extend onto each end of unglued long side; see Diagram 3. Glue fabric ends to unglued side. Fold excess fabric to bottom of box, clipping corners to eliminate bulk; glue. Allow glue to set, then remove masking tape. Set box aside.

5. Place one 7" x 9" box jacket piece on work surface. Coat top surface with glue. Place second 7" x 9" box jacket piece on top, matching edges. If needed, trim edges flush with utility knife, being careful not to alter measurements. Repeat with remaining 7" x 9" box jacket pieces and two 3" x 9" box jacket pieces.

6. Place box jacket covering right side down on work surface. Using dressmaker's pen, T-

45

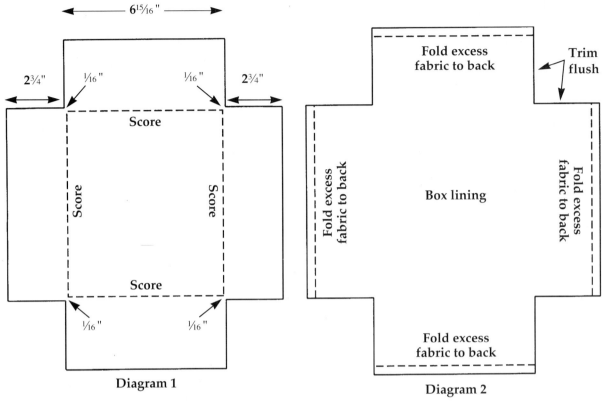

Diagram 1

Diagram 2

square and triangle, measure, mark and draw placement lines on fabric; see Diagram 4.

7. Coat one surface of one 7" x 9" box jacket piece with glue. Make sure fingers are free of glue before handling fabric. Position piece in Block A of box jacket covering, aligning edges with lines. Smooth fabric over piece. Repeat with 3" x 9" box jacket piece in Block B of box jacket covering. Repeat with remaining 7" x 9" box jacket piece in Block C of box jacket covering. Fold excess fabric to un- glued side of box jacket, trimming corners for smooth fit. Glue.

8. Select Block A to be the box lid. Coat uncovered side with glue. Make sure fingers are free of glue before handling fabric. Center box jacket lining on lid and smooth

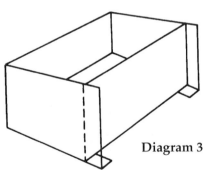

Diagram 3

into place; bottom section of lining will extend about 1" over Block B. Glue lining extension to Block B, creating a soft hinge; see Diagram 5. Carefully remove any excess glue before it sets. Weight box jacket with books until completely dry.

9. Coat bottom of box with glue. Position box on Block C of box jacket, horizontally

46

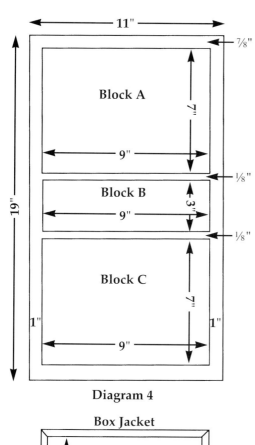

Diagram 4

centered and with bottom edge of uncovered side aligned with box jacket fold; see Diagram 6. Press in place; allow to dry. Coat uncovered side of box with glue and press Block B to glued surface. Check to make sure lid aligns with box opening, then tape Block B in place until glue sets.

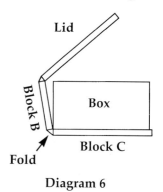

Diagram 6

10. To make tray, measure, mark, cut and score tray piece; see Diagram 7. Do not fold. Repeat Step 2, using tray piece and tray lining. Using tray covering, repeat Step 3, covering all four sides of tray and folding

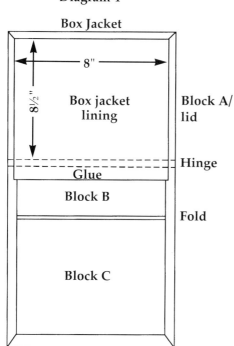

Diagram 5

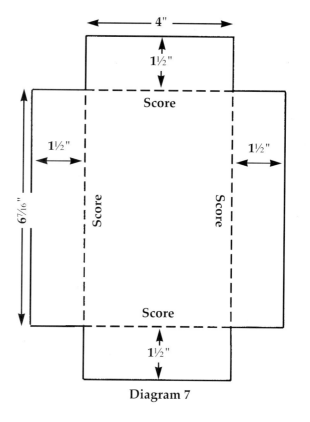

Diagram 7

about 1" of excess fabric to bottom of tray. Center and glue tray underside to bottom of tray.

11. To make divider, measure and mark cardboard; see Diagram 8. Score along Lines A and B. Do not fold. Turn divider over and score along Line C. Place divider with scored Lines A and B down on work surface. Glue divider covering over cardboard, folding excess fabric to back. Allow glue to set for 5 minutes. Fold along scores. Glue Section 1 to Section 2; see Diagram 8. Insert divider into tray, gluing if desired.

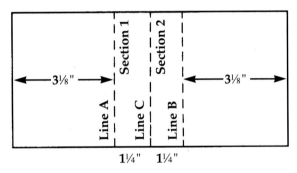

Diagram 8

The lid of the Keepsake Box may be decorated in many ways. Cross-stitched initials or other small cross-stitched motifs, such as those from the "Holiday Wreath Jar Lids" on page 21, may be placed on the lid. Cut a piece of fleece or flannel slightly smaller than the design. Glue this to the lid first, then center the cross-stitched piece over it and glue the edges down. Cover raw edges with ribbon, flat braid, lace or gold cord.

Try This

The lid of the Keepsake Box may be decorated in many ways. Cross-stitched initials or other small cross-stitched motifs, such as those from the "Holiday Wreath Jar Lids" on page 21, may be placed on the lid. Cut a piece of fleece or flannel slightly smaller than the design. Glue this to the lid first, then center the cross-stitched piece over it and glue the edges down. Cover raw edges with ribbon, flat braid, lace or gold cord.

To delight the Victorian, glue on a bouquet of tiny dried flowers accented with wired ribbon. For a Christmas touch, add a cluster of small pinecones, silk holly and red ribbons. For Thanksgiving, add silk or wooden fruits and berries.

Glue a favorite photo or postcard to the center of the lid. Cut a slightly larger piece of clear Mylar; center it over the picture. Glue Mylar edges in place, then cover edges with ribbon or flat decorative braid.

The fabric chosen can help pinpoint a theme: a Southwestern pattern, a floral, a country gingham, an elegant brocade, an animal print or cartoon character print may give you ideas for lid decoration.

Opposite: Grand Gingerbread Sweatshirt

Grand Gingerbread Sweatshirt

There are no calories in the sweet treats appliquéd on this shirt! (Project pictured on previous page.)

MATERIALS

Purchased forest green sweatshirt
⅛ yard of brown fabric; matching thread
Scrap of tan fabric; matching thread
Scrap of red fabric
Scrap of gold fabric
12" x 14" piece of paper-backed fusible webbing
¼ yard of fusible tear-away
⅝ yard of ¼"-wide white rickrack
Hot glue gun and glue sticks
Eight 3mm faceted black beads
Four 3mm brown beads
One hundred fifty #00968 Mill Hill seed beads*
#9 embroidery needle
Dressmaker's pen
Twelve assorted small buttons

*See "Suppliers" on page 128.

DIRECTIONS

1. Trace gingerbread man, heart and star patterns on page 51. On paper side of fusible webbing, draw four gingerbread men, three hearts and one star, leaving at least ½" between each. Cut out, leaving space between each. Do not remove paper. Fuse rough side of three gingerbread men to wrong side of brown fabric; iron. Repeat with remaining gingerbread man on tan fabric, hearts on red fabric and star on gold fabric. Cut out appliqués. Remove paper.

2. Position one brown gingerbread appliqué webbing side down 1" below center of right shoulder seam of sweatshirt. Fuse. Position tan gingerbread appliqué with top of head centered 1" below feet of first appliqué; fuse. Repeat with remaining gingerbread appliqués. Position one heart webbing side down on each brown gingerbread appliqué and star on tan gingerbread appliqué; see diagram. Fuse.

Diagram

3. From tear-away, cut one 6" x 25" strip. Turn sweatshirt inside out. Place shiny side of tear-away against wrong side of sweatshirt aligned behind vertical row of gingerbread men. Iron. Turn sweatshirt right side out. Cut rickrack into desired lengths to decorate gingerbread men; see diagram. Glue. Using thread to match gingerbread men, finish edges of appliqués with machine satin stitching. To remove tear-away, lift at one corner and carefully tear. To remove from appliqués, make a small scissor cut in tear-away backing appliqués; lift and tear.

4. Sew two black beads on each gingerbread man for eyes. Sew one brown bead on each gingerbread man for nose. To make a mouth, draw a smile on one gingerbread man face; see diagram. Cut one 7" length of brown thread; knot one end. Using embroidery needle and starting at one end of smile, bring needle from wrong side of sweatshirt to right side and string one seed bead onto thread. Bring needle to wrong side and back to right side then

thread second bead and repeat. Repeat until smile is completed, adjusting number of beads as needed. Repeat for remaining gingerbread men. Sew three buttons on front of each gingerbread man as desired.

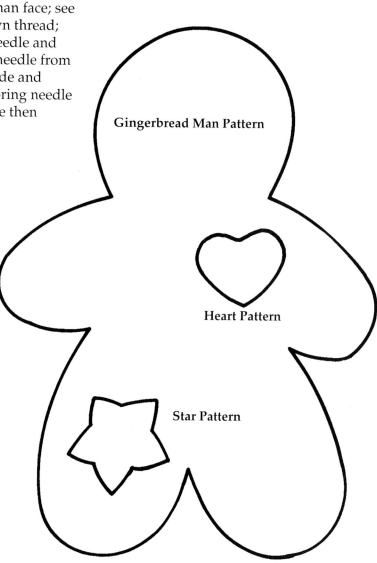

Gingerbread Man Pattern

Heart Pattern

Star Pattern

Sweet Christmas Sachet

White and gold sparkle on this fragrant sachet, wonderful to have or to give.

MATERIALS

¼ yard of 2½"-wide ivory grosgrain ribbon
Eight spools of Balger metallic thread
  (Solid Gold 2000)*
Embroidery needle
9" x 10" piece of ivory taffeta; matching thread
Scraps of batting
1 ounce of potpourri
¾ yard of ⅛"-wide flat gold braid
½ yard of gold cord
Hot glue gun and glue sticks

*See "Suppliers" on page 128.

DIRECTIONS
All seams are ¼".

1. Using metallic thread and embroidery pattern opposite, stitch seven flowers ½" apart on grosgrain ribbon, aligning tops with long edge and placing first flower ½" from one end of ribbon. Flower centers are French knots; leaves and petals are lazy daisy stitch; see "General Instructions" on page 126. Repeat along opposite edge of ribbon, staggering motifs. Set aside.

Embroidery Pattern

2. Make two 3¼"-long tassels from metallic thread; see "General Instructions" on page 126.

3. Hem short edges of taffeta by turning under 1"; press lightly. With right sides facing, sew long edges together. Turn.

4. Sew gathering thread ½" below ends of taffeta tube.

5. Wrap potpourri in batting scrap until it fits snugly when inserted inside taffeta tube.

6. Tighten gathering threads; secure. Tack one tassel to each end of sachet.

7. Measure around middle of sachet, subtracting ¼" to achieve snug fit. With right sides facing, sew ends of grosgrain ribbon together to equal measurement. Turn. Slide band onto sachet, matching seams. Glue gold braid and gold cord to ribbon as desired; see photo.

Softy the Snowman Stocking

Soft as a fresh snowfall, this winter-crisp and cheerful stocking adds a contemporary note to your Christmas decorations.

MATERIALS

1 yard of white broadcloth
½ yard of white organdy
⅛ yard of white felt
¼ yard of dark green felt
Scrap of peach felt
Scrap of dark gray felt
¼ yards of ¼"-wide cording
⅛ yard of metallic green fabric; matching thread
Tracing paper
Dressmaker's pen
18" x 12" sheet of paper-backed fusible webbing
Embroidery floss: black, red, green, peach

DIRECTIONS

All seams are ½".

1. Trace snowman patterns on page 56, transferring all information. Enlarge stocking pattern on page 57; see "General Instructions" on page 126; set patterns aside.

2. From broadcloth, cut four 14" x 18" pieces. From organdy, cut two 14" x 18" pieces. For stocking hanger, cut one 1½" x 3" strip from green fabric; set aside. Also from green fabric, cut 2½"-wide bias strips, piecing as needed to equal 1¼ yards. Make 1¼ yards of corded piping; see "General Instructions" on page 126. Set aside.

3. Using dressmaker's pen and making very light marks, transfer stocking outline to all broadcloth pieces. Then transfer snowman

outline to one stocking shape, centering it horizontally, with top of hat 1½" below top edge of stocking shape. Place one snowman on each side of the first snowman, with about ½" between each body.

4. Fuse rough side of fusible webbing to wrong side of felt. Do not remove paper. Transfer snowman hat pattern to paper side of dark gray felt; draw three hats. Transfer scarf pattern to paper side of dark green felt; draw three scarves. Reverse and transfer stocking heel and toe outlines to paper side of dark green felt; draw one of each. Transfer snowman head and body patterns to paper side of patterns to paper side of white felt; draw three of each. Transfer nose pattern to paper side of peach felt; draw three noses. Cut out shapes. Remove paper.

5. With webbing side down, position snowman pieces on snowman outlines on stocking shape. Fuse. Place noses in position on snowman faces; fuse. Fuse green felt heel and toe pieces in place on stocking shape; see photo.

6. Matching all edges, place one organdy piece over stocking shape with snowmen, heel and toe on it. Smooth fabrics; baste edges together. To outline snowmen, use single strand of black floss to quilt through broadcloth and organdy close to, but not touching, felt pieces. To stitch details on scarves, use single strand of green floss; see photo. Use single strand of black to stitch

55

arms and single strand of peach to outline noses.

7. Make five French knots with black floss for each mouth and three with red floss for holly berries on each hat; see "General Instructions" on page 126. For holly leaves, use fern stitch with green floss; see Diagram 1. For snowman buttons, make three Smyrna crosses each with black floss; see Diagram 2. For eyes, make one single-strand cross-stitch with black floss for each eye; see photo.

8. Decorate heel and toe "seams" with French knots in red floss and feather stitching in green floss. See "General Instructions" on page 126 for feather stitching diagram. Cut out stocking front according to pattern. Remove basting.

9. With right sides facing and edges aligned, sew green piping to stocking front.

10. To finish stocking back, pin together one broadcloth stocking piece and remaining organdy stocking piece. With organdy sides facing, sew stocking back to assembled stocking front along stitching line of piping, leaving top open. Turn.

11. To make stocking hanger, fold 1½"-wide green fabric strip in half lengthwise with right sides facing, and sew long edges together. Turn. Press to make ½"-wide hanger. Fold hanger in half. Align raw edges with stocking top on heel side; baste in place.

12. To finish lining, sew remaining broadcloth stocking pieces together with right sides facing, leaving opening at top and in seam above heel. Do not turn. Slide lining over stocking, matching seams and top edges. Sew seam around stocking top, securing stocking

hanger in seam. Turn through opening in lining above heel. Slipstitch opening closed. Tuck lining inside stocking.

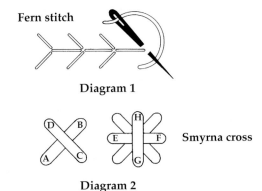

Fern stitch

Diagram 1

Smyrna cross

Diagram 2

Snowman Patterns

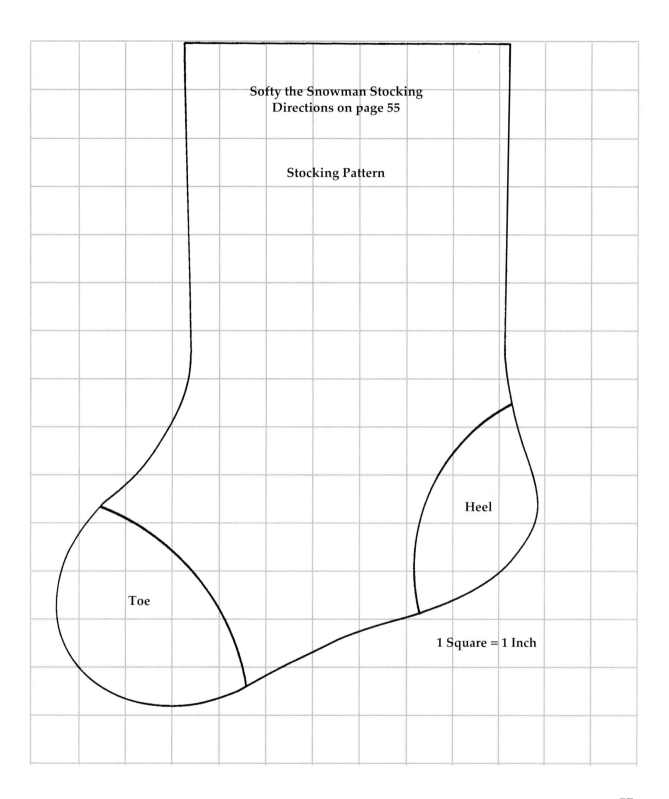

Softy the Snowman Stocking
Directions on page 55

Stocking Pattern

Heel

Toe

1 Square = 1 Inch

Christmas Beauty Paperweight

A simple cross-stitched motif inspired by the hues and shapes of traditional holly turns a coaster into an heirloom paperweight.

MODEL

Stitched on cream Aida 18 over one thread, the finished design size is 2⅛" x 2⅞". The fabric was cut 6" x 6".

FABRICS   DESIGN SIZES

FABRICS	DESIGN SIZES
Aida 11	3½" x 4¾"
Aida 14	2¾" x 3¾"
Hardanger 22	1¾" x 2⅜"

MATERIALS

Completed design piece on cream Aida 18
Purchased wooden coaster with glass insert*
One 4½" x 4½" piece of ¼"-thick Styrofoam
Craft knife
Hot glue gun and glue sticks

*See "Suppliers" on page 128.

DIRECTIONS

1. Remove glass insert from coaster base. Using insert's rim as pattern, cut Styrofoam into circle. Trim circle ⅛" all around.

2. Center design piece on Styrofoam. Fold excess fabric to back, trimming as needed for smooth fit. Glue. Center and glue design piece inside coaster base.

3. Replace glass insert upside down in coaster base to form cover over design piece.

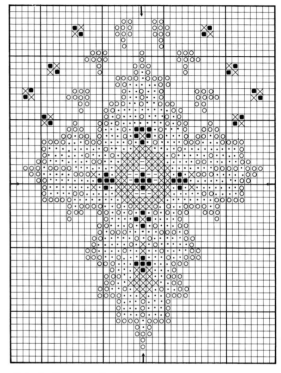

Stitch Count: 39 x 52

Anchor		DMC (used for sample)	
		Step 1: Cross-stitch (2 strands)	
891	–	676	Old Gold-lt.
19	X	817	Coral Red-vy. dk.
118	■	340	Blue Violet-med.
975	O	3753	Antique Blue-vy. lt.
862	·	520	Fern Green-dk.

Picture a Pretty Frame

This lace-embellished frame could be a keepsake from days gone by, but you can make it today and show off a treasured photograph.

MATERIALS

Two purchased 8" x 10" precut mats with matching windows
One 20" x 20" piece of mat board
Dressmaker's pen
⅜ yard of floral fabric; matching thread
Assorted lace scraps and doilies
½ yard of ⅛"-wide antique violet silk ribbon
½ yard of ⅛"-wide taupe silk ribbon
½ yard of ⅛"-wide rose silk ribbon
½ yard of ⅛"-wide deep rose silk ribbon
½ yard of ⅛"-wide sage silk ribbon
½ yard of ⅛"-wide gray-blue silk ribbon
Pink and lavender embroidery floss
Large-eyed needle
Hot glue gun and glue sticks
Seven small buttons
Assorted metallic seed beads and faux pearls
Gold rose charm with three leaf bunches
Two gold branch and leaf charms
⅜ yard of 1"-wide crochet trim
Tracing paper
⅜ yard of fleece
Craft knife
Permanent spray adhesive
Tacky glue
Glue brush or roller
Craft knife
⅜ yard of ⅝"-wide black silk ribbon
½ yard of black velvet
¼ yard of black broadcloth
⅞ yard of ¼"-wide green silk braid
1⅛ yards of ¼"-wide flat gold trim

DIRECTIONS

1. From floral fabric, cut one 10" x 12" piece. Center one precut mat on right side of fabric. Using dressmaker's pen, outline window and edges of mat, marking 1" seam allowance inside window and along edges. Trim fabric to seam allowance at edges. Do not cut out window. Sew or hot-glue lace scraps to fabric, one layer at a time as desired. Cut doilies in half to make draped shapes; see photo. Trim lace and doily edges to match seam allowances in window and on edges.

2. This step contains specifics for accenting the lace-covered frame with ribbon work, buttons, beads and charms; see Embellishment Diagram and Color Key on page 62 for stitching and color placement.

  A. To make flower at lower left corner of window, draw a ½"-diameter circle on fabric according to "E" on Embellishment Diagram. Using various stitch lengths and overlapping some stitches, complete half of flower using antique violet ribbon; see Diagram 1. Complete remaining half using taupe ribbon. Using rose ribbon,

Diagram 1

61

Embellishment Diagram

A, B, C, D = Ribbon cascade
E = Flower
F = Ribbon rosebud
⊗ = Faux pearl
● = Button
▦ = Gold Charm
◄ = Leaf
▭ = Bullion stitch petal
○ = Bead

Color Key
A = Antique violet, taupe, rose, antique violet
B = Rose, antique violet
C = Taupe, rose
D = Antique violet, taupe, rose
E = Antique violet, taupe, rose
F = Deep rose
Leaves = Sage, gray-blue
Bullion stitch petals = Rose, lavender

make flower center with single stitch; stitch additional petals below taupe ribbon.

B. To make ribbon cascades, draw curved lines on fabric according to Embellishment Diagram. Satin-stitch along each line, varying stitch width and alternating colors according to Color Key.

C. To make a ribbon rose-bud, cut a 3" length of deep rose ribbon. Draw ribbon up through fabric then back down, making a ¼" loop. Bring ribbon back up through fabric at center of loop and down again ⅛" from center; see Diagram 2.

Diagram 2

D. To make a bullion stitch petal, use two strands of floss. Place petals below rosebuds. Bring needle up at 1, then down at 2, keeping floss loose; see Diagram 3A. Bring needle tip out again at 1, but do not pull needle completely through fabric; see Diagram 3A. Wrap loose stitched floss around needle tip thirteen times; see Diagram 3B. Holding finger over wrapped area, pull needle through floss; see

Diagram 3C. Insert needle again at 2, pulling to fabric back; see Diagram 3D. If desired, pull floss slightly to curve bullion petal.

E. To make a leaf, make single stitch with ribbon, twisting it slightly to resemble a leaf.

F. Sew beads, buttons and faux pearls to fabric. Hot-glue leaf bunches to fabric at lower left and rose charm to fabric at upper right.

3. Center one precut mat on fleece. Outline window and edges of mat. Trim fleece to match mat. From mat board, cut one piece same size as precut mats for frame back. Also cut one piece ¼" smaller for backing piece. Set aside frame back and backing piece.

4. Place one precut mat on work surface. Spray thin coat of adhesive on front. Smooth fleece onto glued surface. Allow glue to set.

5. Spray fleece with thin coat of adhesive. Make sure fingers are free of adhesive before handling fabric. Center fabric right side up over fleece, matching edge and window outlines. Smooth fabric onto fleece. Allow to set. Cut out window in fabric along line of seam allowance. Clip corners. Fold fabric on one edge of window and on opposite outside edge firmly to back of mat board, keeping tension even. Trim corners as needed for smooth fit. Secure with tacky glue. Repeat with

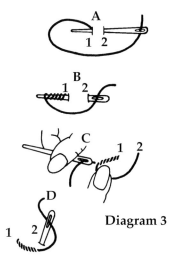

Diagram 3

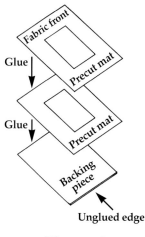

Diagram 4

remaining edges. Place precut mat fabric side down on clean work surface. Hot-glue crochet trim along right and bottom edges of window, allowing ½" to show. Matching edges, use tacky glue to attach remaining precut mat to back of fabric-covered mat; see Diagram 4.

6. From black velvet, cut two 9" x 11" pieces; set one aside for frame back cover. Place backing piece on work surface. Spray with thin coat of adhesive. Center one 9" x 11" velvet piece over backing piece; smooth in place. Fold excess fabric to back, trimming corners to eliminate bulk. Glue.

7. To assemble frame front, spread tacky glue on back of precut mat to within 1" of window, leaving bottom edge open so that photograph may be inserted in frame; see Diagram 4. Do not allow glue to spread into window. Center backing piece over back of precut mat so velvet shows in window; press in place.

8. Enlarge pattern for stand on page 66, transferring all information; see "General Instructions" on page 126. From mat board, cut one stand according to pattern and two stands ¹⁄₁₆" smaller. From black velvet, cut one stand cover, adding 1" seam allowance on sides and bottom edge of stand pattern and 1¼" seam allowance on top edge. From broadcloth, cut one stand cover, adding 1" seam allowance to stand pattern on all edges. Using craft knife, make slit in large stand, small stands and broadcloth stand cover according to pattern. From black ribbon, cut two 6" lengths and one 1" length.

9. Place large stand right side down on clean work surface. Insert 1" of one 6" length of black ribbon through slit; see Diagram 5. Hot-glue ribbon end to stand back. Turn stand so

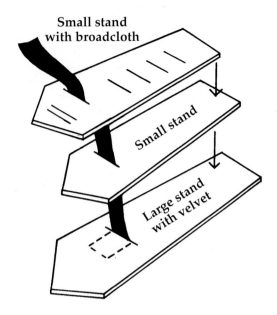

Diagram 5

ribbon tail hangs free. Note which side of one small stand aligns with ribbon tail side of large stand. Coat opposite side with spray adhesive. Center one small stand on large stand front, aligning slits. Draw ribbon tail through slit in small stand; see Diagram 5. Glue stands together. Place under heavy book and allow to set.

10. With ribbon tail underneath, place stand on work surface. Coat lightly with spray adhesive. Position velvet stand cover wrong side down over stand, leaving 1¼" allowance extending above top of stand. Smooth velvet onto stand. Fold velvet to back along all edges except top, trimming corners as needed for smooth fit; glue with tacky glue.

11. Before covering remaining small mat board stand, note which side aligns with ribbon tail side of velvet stand. Coat opposite side with spray adhesive. Center small stand on wrong side of broadcloth stand cover, aligning slits. Smooth broadcloth onto stand. Fold broadcloth to back of stand along all edges, trimming corners as needed for smooth fit; glue with tacky glue. Center small broadcloth stand over ribbon tail side of velvet stand with uncovered sides facing. Draw ribbon through slit in broadcloth stand; see Diagram 5. Using tacky glue, glue together uncoated sides of velvet stand and broadcloth stand. Place under heavy book and allow to set.

12. Using craft knife, slit frame back cover and mat board frame back according to pattern. Place frame back right side up on work surface. Place stand in position to ensure that slits in frame back align with cut in stand and with top edge of stand; see Diagram 6. Remove stand. Coat frame back lightly with spray adhesive. Center frame back on wrong side of frame back cover, aligning slits. Smooth cover in place. Fold velvet to back, trimming corners as needed for smooth fit; glue with tacky glue. Fold under edges of velvet extending from top of stand, and insert fabric into larger slit on frame back so stand top rests against frame back; see Diagram 7. Insert 1" of the ribbon extending from stand into smaller cut. Glue velvet and ribbon ends to back of frame back. Double remaining 6" ribbon length so that short ends overlap slightly in center of loop. Glue ends together. Flatten loop into bow. Fold 1" ribbon length around bow center. Glue ends together under bow. Glue bow to stand top with glued ends underneath.

13. Using tacky glue, glue uncovered side of frame back securely to back of assembled frame front. From silk braid, cut a 30" length. Glue along side and top edges of backing piece portion of frame front, allowing braid to

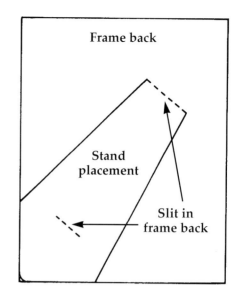

Diagram 6

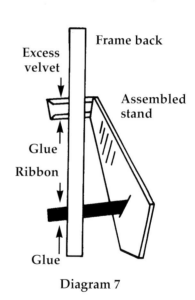

Diagram 7

extend ½" around each bottom corner. Trim excess. Glue gold trim along edge of precut mats, butting silk braid. Trim excess.

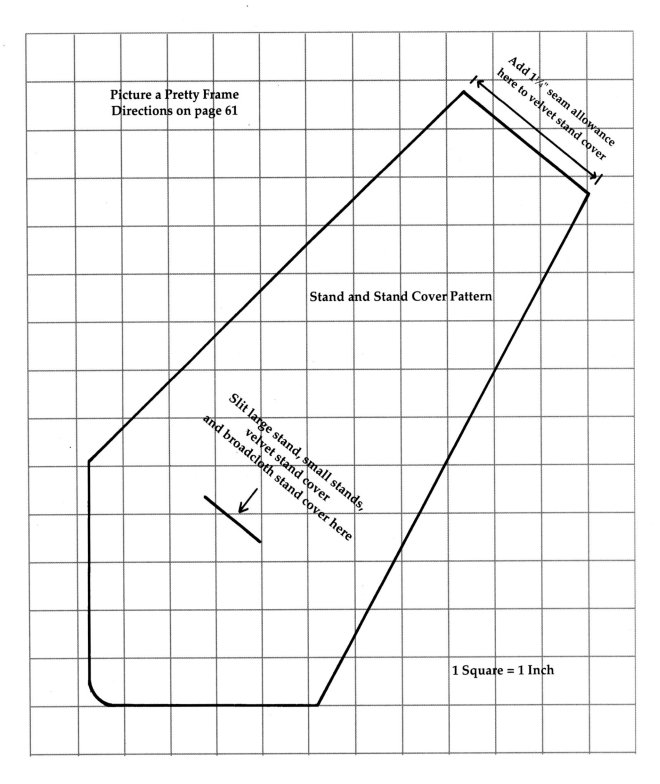

Picture a Pretty Frame
Directions on page 61

Stand and Stand Cover Pattern

Add 1¼" seam allowance here to velvet stand cover

Slit large stand, small stands, velvet stand cover and broadcloth stand cover here

1 Square = 1 Inch

Opposite: Hearts 'n' Flowers Mat

Hearts 'n' Flowers Mat

Imprinted with Christmas colors, this sturdy canvas mat may be used on a floor or tabletop or as a wallhanging. (Project pictured on previous page.)

MATERIALS

One 37" x 29" piece of heavy canvas
Fabric glue
Scissors
Tracing paper
Scraps of mat board
One package of adhesive-backed moleskin
Craft knife
Four pushpins
Hot glue gun and glue sticks
Chalk-A-Line marker (available at
    craft stores)
Acrylic paints: red, green
Two small, shallow bowls
Newspapers
Water-base varnish and brush

DIRECTIONS

1. Fold edges of canvas under 1½". Iron flat, if necessary. Trim canvas on back to make mitered corners; see Diagram 1. Glue edges down, using fabric glue.

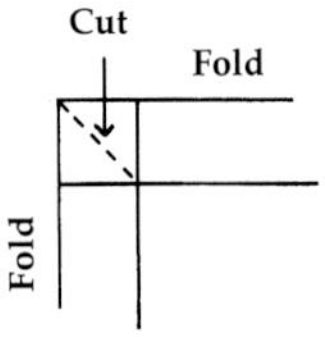

Diagram 1

2. Trace block, flower bud, flower stem and heart patterns on page 125. From moleskin, cut one of each; do not remove backing. Also cut one of each from mat board.

3. Remove backing from moleskin block; adhere to mat board block. Stick a pushpin in center of mat board side of pattern; do not push point all the way through. Repeat with remaining shapes.

4. Place canvas right side up on flat surface. Using Chalk-A-Line marker, draw a line 2⅛" from and parallel to right long edge of canvas. Draw a second line 4⅛" from and parallel to the same edge. Repeat with the other three edges of canvas. Mark off 2" blocks along each edge; see Diagram 2 for placement.

5. Pour green paint into one bowl. Spread newspaper beside bowl. Using pushpin as handle, carefully dip moleskin surface only of block pattern piece into paint. Stamp block once, gently, on newspaper to remove excess paint. Imprint green block in second square to the left on bottom edge of canvas, with top of block on marked line; see Diagram 2. Continue imprinting green squares around canvas, following marked lines and dipping pattern piece into paint as needed. See Diagram 2 for placement. Allow to dry.

6. Using pushpin as handle, carefully dip moleskin surface only of flower stem pattern piece into green paint. Remove excess paint as in Step 5. Imprint flower stem in center of alternating unpainted squares on canvas, dipping pattern piece into paint as needed. See Diagram 2 for placement. Allow to dry.

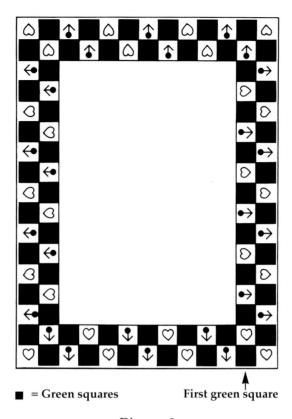

■ = Green squares

First green square

Diagram 2

7. Pour red paint into second bowl. Spread fresh newspaper beside bowl. Using pushpin as handle, carefully dip moleskin surface only of flower bud pattern piece into paint. Remove excess paint as in Step 5. Imprint one flower bud above each flower stem, dipping pattern piece into paint as needed. See Diagram 2 for placement. Allow to dry.

8. Using pushpin as handle, carefully dip moleskin surface only of heart pattern piece into red paint. Remove excess paint as in Step 5. Imprint one heart in center of remaining unpainted squares on canvas, dipping pattern piece into paint as needed. Allow to dry.

9. If mat is to be used on the floor or wall, cover entire front surface with one coat of varnish. Varnish will slightly darken the canvas. Allow to dry.

69

Radiant Roses Throw

Delicate roses adorn this luxurious velveteen throw. Embellish it with handmade tassels.

MATERIALS (for throw)

2 yards of cream cotton velveteen; matching thread
2 yards of floral print fabric; matching thread
Tracing paper
Soft lead pencil
Craft knife
7" x 9" sheet of frosted Mylar
8" x 10" piece of mat board
Drafting tape
Stencil Magic Paint Cream*: Jungle Green, Pink Carnation
One ⅛"-diameter stencil brush
Small paintbrush
6¼ yards of ⅛"-wide dusty rose drapery piping
1⅞ yards of variegated pink/green wired ribbon
Eight ⅜"-diameter pink, rose-shaped shank buttons

*See "Suppliers" on page 128.

DIRECTIONS
All seams are ½".

1. Using soft lead pencil, trace rose, leaf and stem pattern on page 73 onto Mylar. Tape corners of Mylar to mat board. Using craft knife, cut out areas of Mylar to be stenciled.

2. From velveteen and floral print fabric, cut one 45" x 63" piece each. Set print fabric aside.

Place velveteen right side up on flat surface. Place stencil in one corner 4½" from short edge and 3⅛" from long edge; see Diagram 1. Using Jungle Green and stencil brush, stencil leaf and stem groups on velveteen. For second motif, turn stencil 90 degrees clockwise and move across width of velveteen 6" away from first motif. Repeat for remainder of first row. Use paintbrush to add green shading to leaves and stems. Using Pink Carnation and stencil brush, stencil roses on velveteen. Use paintbrush to add pink shading. Repeat for remaining area of velveteen, with five rows of three motifs each. Allow stenciled fabric to dry flat for two days.

3. With right sides facing, sew dusty rose drapery piping to velveteen, beginning ½" from one end of piping and rounding corners. Start and end piping in same corner; see Diagram 2. Trim excess, leaving ½" tail. Tack tails together to make smooth joint; see Diagram 2. With right sides facing, sew velveteen and print fabric together along stitching line of piping, leaving an opening. Turn. Slipstitch opening closed.

4. To make ribbon rosettes, cut pink/green wired ribbon into eight 8" lengths. Sew a gathering thread along one long edge of each length. Gather thread tightly; secure. Arrange ribbon for ruffled effect. Tack rosettes to throw as desired, sewing through both layers of fabric; see photo. Tack one pink button in center of each rosette.

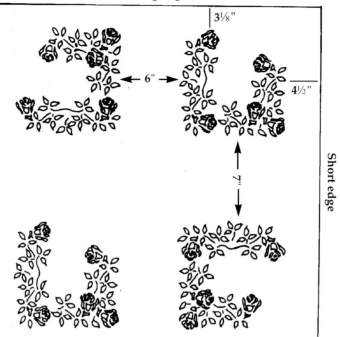

Long edge

3⅛"

← 6" →

4½"

Short edge

7"

Diagram 1

MATERIALS (for one tassel)

1½ skeins of burgundy pearl cotton size 3
1½ skeins of deep rose pearl cotton size 3
6" x 6" piece of cardboard
Cellophane tape
Scissors
4" x 1½" piece of rose velveteen; matching
   thread
¼ yard of ¾"-wide variegated green wired
   ribbon
⅛ yard of ¾"-wide pink wired ribbon

DIRECTIONS

1. Using burgundy and deep rose pearl
cotton, make tassel; see "General Instructions"
on page 126.

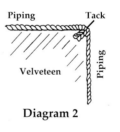

Piping   Tack

Velveteen

Piping

Diagram 2

Diagram 3

2. With right sides facing, sew together short
ends of velveteen. Turn. Fold under one long
edge and sew gathering thread near fold. Do
not cut thread. Slip velveteen tube, gathered
side up, over top of tassel. Tighten gathering
thread and secure. Gather bottom edge of
velveteen tube and secure to tassel, easing
fullness; see Diagram 3.

3. To make ruffle, shape variegated green wired ribbon into a circle. Sew a gathering thread along one edge; do not cut. Slip ribbon down over top of tassel. Position gathered edge over bottom edge of velveteen. Tighten gathering thread and secure. Tack gathered edge of ruffle to velveteen and tassel.

4. Wrap tassel once with pink wired ribbon, covering gathered edge of ruffle. On next wrap, twist ribbon loosely. Tack ribbon end to velveteen and tassel. Make three more tassels by repeating Steps 1–4. Tack one tassel to each corner of throw.

Rose, Leaf and Stem Pattern

Glad Tidings Tea Set Coasters

A hot cup of tea provides a welcome break from the holiday rush. Add these delightful coasters to your teatime arrangements!

MODELS

Stitched on moss green Murano 30 over two threads, the finished design size is 3¾" x 3¾" for each coaster. The fabric was cut 8" x 8".

FABRICS	DESIGN SIZES
Aida 11	5⅛" x 5⅛"
Aida 14	4⅛" x 4⅛"
Aida 18	3⅛" x 3⅛"
Hardanger 22	2⅝" x 2⅝"

MATERIALS (for one coaster)

Completed design piece on moss green
  Murano; matching thread
¼ yard of green print fabric
½ yard of ⅛"-wide cording
¼ yard of fleece

DIRECTIONS
All seams are ¼".

1. With design centered "on point," trim design piece to 4½" x 4½". From fleece and green print fabric, cut 1¼"-wide bias strips, piecing as needed to equal ½ yard. Make ½ yard of corded piping; see "General Instructions" on page 126. With right sides facing and raw edges aligned, sew piping to design piece; trim excess.

2. Baste fleece to wrong side of design piece. With right sides facing, sew green fabric to design piece along stitching line of piping, leaving an opening. Trim fleece from seam allowance. Turn. Slipstitch opening closed.

Anchor	DMC (used for sample)		

Step 1: Cross-stitch (2 strands)

Anchor			DMC	(used for sample)
1	·	⁄·		White
10	✕		352	Coral-lt.
11	■		3328	Salmon-dk.
75	O		3733	Dusty Rose-lt.
76	∴		3731	Dusty Rose-med.
20	●		498	Christmas Red-dk.
216	−		367	Pistachio Green-dk.
879	☐		890	Pistachio Green-ultra dk.
936	▲		632	Pecan-dk.

Step 2: Backstitch (1 strand)

879		890	Pistachio Green-ultra dk.

Step 3: French Knot (1 strand)

879	●	890	Pistachio Green-ultra dk.

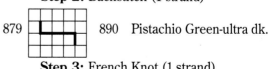

Glad Tidings Tea Set Coasters Graphs
Directions on page 75

Anchor   **DMC (used for sample)**

Step 1: Cross-stitch (2 strands)

1	· / ·	White
10	✕ / ✕	352 Coral-lt.
11	■ / ■	3328 Salmon-dk.
75	○ / ◦	3733 Dusty Rose-lt.
76	∴ / ∴	3731 Dusty Rose-med.
20	● / ●	498 Christmas Red-dk.

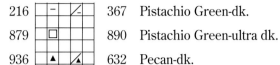

216	- / -	367 Pistachio Green-dk.
879	□	890 Pistachio Green-ultra dk.
936	▲ / ▲	632 Pecan-dk.

Step 2: Backstitch (1 strand)

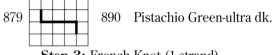

879		890 Pistachio Green-ultra dk.

Step 3: French Knot (1 strand)

879	●	890 Pistachio Green-ultra dk.

Stitch Count: 57 x 57

Glad Tidings Tea Set Coasters Graphs
Directions on page 75

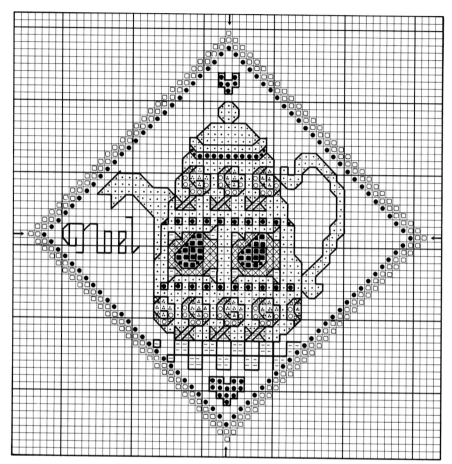

Stitch Count: 57 x 57

Glad Tidings Tea Set Coasters Graphs
Directions on page 75

Anchor   **DMC (used for sample)**

Step 1: Cross-stitch (2 strands)

1	·	⟋	White
10	✕	⟋	352 Coral-lt.
11	■	⟋	3328 Salmon-dk.
75	○	⟋	3733 Dusty Rose-lt.
76	∴	⟋	3731 Dusty Rose-med.
20	●	⟋	498 Christmas Red-dk.

216	–	⟋	367 Pistachio Green-dk.
879	□		890 Pistachio Green-ultra dk.
936	▲	⟋	632 Pecan-dk.

Step 2: Backstitch (1 strand)

879	⌐	890 Pistachio Green-ultra dk.

Step 3: French Knot (1 strand)

879	●	890 Pistachio Green-ultra dk.

Stitch Count: 57 x 57

Glad Tidings Tea Set Coasters Graphs
Directions on page 75

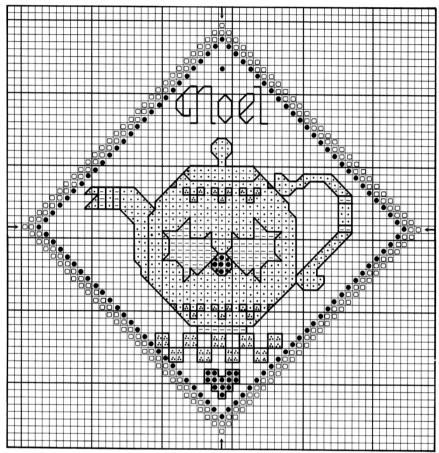

Stitch Count: 57 x 57

Holiday Wheels Pull Toy

This colorful and jolly wooden Santa will roll merrily through many Christmases to come!

MATERIALS

Tracing paper
Pencil
Two 8½" x 11" sheets of graphite paper
One 11" x 8" piece of ¾"-thick wood
Scroll saw, band saw or saber saw
Drill with 5/16" bit
Medium-grit sandpaper
Assorted Delta acrylic paints* (see Color Key on page 84)
Paintbrushes
Acrylic matte-finish spray

Four 1¾"-diameter wooden wheels (available at craft and hobby stores)
One ¼"-diameter dowel
Hot glue gun and glue sticks
¼"-diameter eyescrew
1⅜ yards of ½"-wide green ribbon
One 1"-long faceted wooden bead
One ¼"-long wooden bead

*See "Suppliers" on page 128.

DIRECTIONS

1. Trace pull toy pattern on pages 82 and 83, transferring all information. Using graphite paper, transfer pattern to one surface of ¾"-thick wood. Using saw, cut out along outline. Drill two holes through sleigh runners according to pattern. Reverse pattern and transfer to other surface of wood, matching pattern outline with cut edges of wood. Lightly smooth edges with sandpaper.

2. From dowel, cut two 2"-long pieces to make axles for wheels. Paint dowels and wheels burnt umber. Allow to dry. Coat with matte-finish acrylic spray and set aside. Paint design on one surface of wood according to color diagram on page 84. Paint black lines and details last. Allow to dry. Coat with matte-finish acrylic spray; allow to dry. Repeat on other surface of wood. Paint edges of wood in appropriate colors according to diagram; allow to dry.

3. Glue one end of one axle into one wheel. Repeat with second wheel and axle. Insert axles through drilled holes in sleigh runners. Before gluing remaining wheels to axles, make sure axles move freely in drilled holes. Glue one remaining wheel to each axle.

4. Twist eyescrew into painted edge of wooden shape on front edge of sleigh. Insert one end of ribbon through eye; tie in a bow. Notch ribbon tail. Insert opposite end of ribbon through faceted bead, then through ¼"-long bead. Double ribbon around bead; knot. Tuck ribbon tail back inside faceted bead.

Holiday Wheels Pull Toy
Directions on page 81

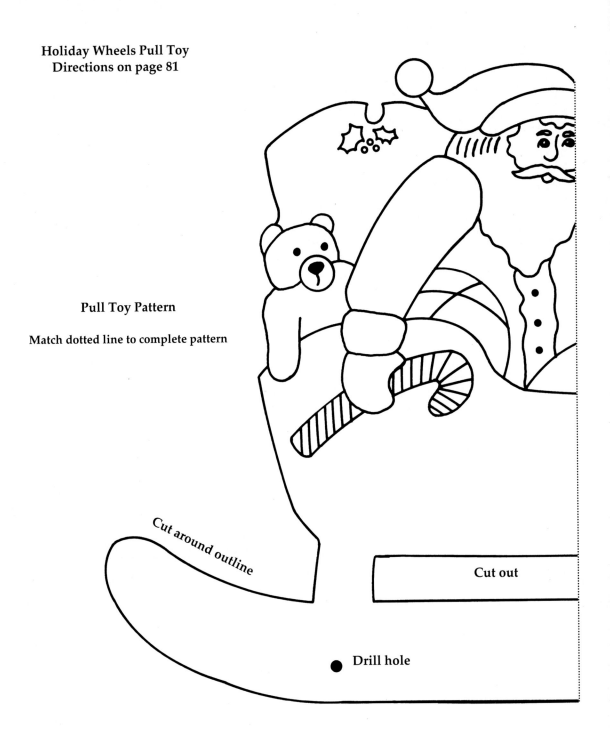

Pull Toy Pattern

Match dotted line to complete pattern

Cut around outline

Cut out

● Drill hole

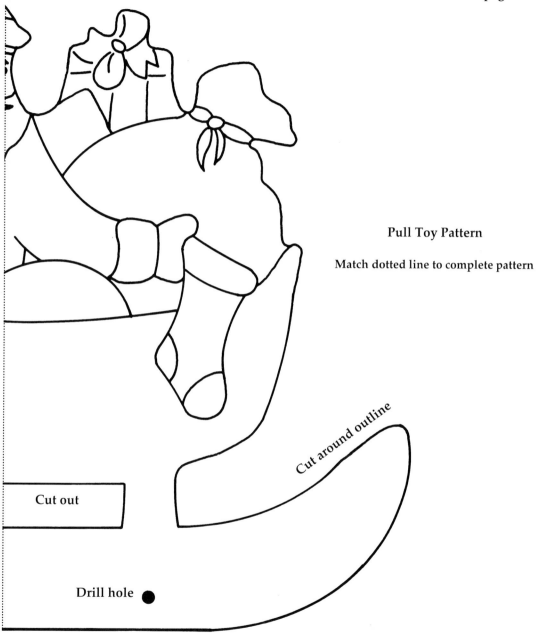

Pull Toy Pattern

Match dotted line to complete pattern

Cut around outline

Cut out

Drill hole ●

Holiday Wheels Pull Toy
Directions on page 81

Color Key
1 = White (shade with Drizzle Gray)
2 = Charcoal (shade with Black)
3 = Territorial Beige (shade with Burnt Umber)
4 = AC Flesh
5 = Fleshtone
6a = Tompe Red
6b = Tompe Red (shade with Mendocino Red)
7 = Coral
8 = Seminole Green (holly veins: Pine Needle Green)
9 = CC Green Apple (shade with Seminole Green)
10 = Butter Yellow
11 = Spice Tan (shade with Spice Brown)

12 = CC Light Coral Bells (shade with Coral)
13 = CC Indian Sky (shade with DA Country Blue)
    (dots: white)
14 = DA Country Blue (shade with CC Royal Blue)
    (dots: Butter Yellow)
15 = Sachet (shade with Medocino Red + White)
16 = CC Purple Canyon + White (shade with CC Purple
Canyon)
17 = Alpine Green (shade with Woodland Night)
18 = Burnt Umber (wheels and axles are also
    Burnt Umber)

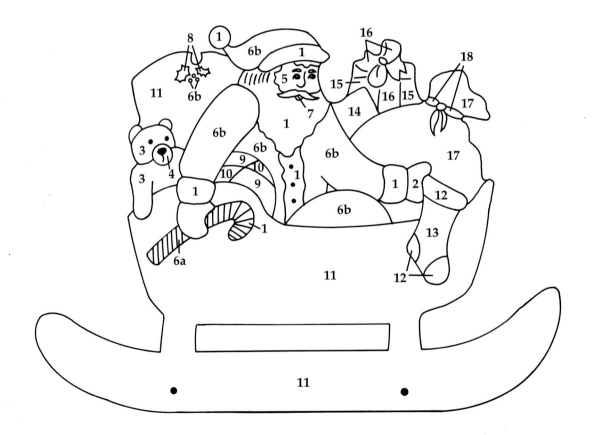

Opposite: Magic Kaleidoscope

agic Kaleidoscope

Aim the end of this easy-to-make kaleidoscope at any light source and watch the colors and patterns swirl and change! (Project pictured on previous page.)

MATERIALS

1¾"-diameter x 8¼"-long mailing tube	Pencil
One 20" x 20" sheet of floral wrapping paper	Craft knife
Spray adhesive	Hot glue gun and glue sticks
Three 1⅛" x 8" single-strength mirrors*	⅜ yard of ½"-wide gold trim
Two 1½"-diameter glass circles*	⅜ yard of ¼"-wide gold trim
Two 1⅝"-diameter glass circles*	10" x 10" piece of bristol board
Strapping tape	Thirty 1mm glass beads in assorted colors
Cellophane tape	Assorted small dried flowers
Dime	

*Mirrors and glass circles to fit any size tube may be purchased from a professional glass cutter.

DIRECTIONS

1. Measure around mailing tube. From wrapping paper, cut one 8¼"-wide piece long enough to fit around mailing tube with a ¼" overlap. Place paper right side down on flat surface. Coat with spray adhesive. Smooth paper around tube.

2. With shiny sides inward, fit mirrors together so that ends form a triangle; see Diagram 1. Secure edges where mirrors meet with strapping tape. Reinforce mirror backs with

strapping tape. Insert mirror triangle ¹⁄₁₆" inside one end of tube; see Diagram 2. Insert one 1½" glass circle into same end of tube to rest on edges of mirror triangle. Secure edges only with cellophane tape. Insert second 1½" glass circle ¹⁄₁₆" inside opposite end of tube. Secure edges only with cellophane tape. See Diagram 3.

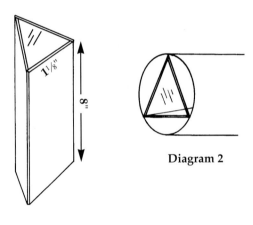

Diagram 2

Diagram 1

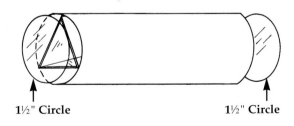

1½" Circle   1½" Circle

Diagram 3

3. From bristol board, cut a 1⅝"-diameter circle. From wrapping paper, cut a matching circle. Glue wrong side of paper circle to bristol board circle, matching edges. With paper side down, center a dime on the circle. Outline dime with pencil. Using craft knife, cut out dime shape for eyehole. Center bristol board side of circle inside one end of tube. Glue to glass circle. Do not allow glue to spread into opening.

4. Cut a length of ½"-wide gold trim long enough to fit around tube. Glue around tube end with eyehole, slightly overlapping edges of paper circle. Wrap cellophane tape around opposite end of mailing tube, slightly overlapping glass circle.

5. To make kaleidoscope end piece, measure around taped end of tube. From bristol board, cut a 3"-wide strip long enough to fit snugly around tube without slipping off, but loose enough so that strip will turn easily. Butt short ends of bristol board strip and tape together securely. Set aside. Cut a 1¼"-wide strip of bristol board 1¾" shorter than end piece. Butt short ends of strip and tape together securely.

6. Measure around kaleidoscope end piece. From wrapping paper, cut a 3½"-wide piece long enough to fit around end piece with a ¼" overlap. Place paper printed side down on work surface. Coat with spray adhesive. Smooth paper around end piece, with ¼" extending over ends. Fold excess to inside of tube and glue in place. Insert small tube into end piece, so one end is almost flush with top edge of end piece; see Diagram 4.

7. Insert one 1⅝"-diameter glass circle inside top of end piece so it rests on edges of small

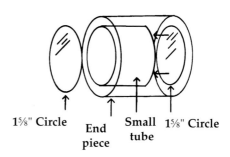

1⅝" Circle   End piece   Small tube   1⅝" Circle

Diagram 4

tube; see Diagram 4. Secure with small beads of glue. Position tube vertically with end piece opening up. Place beads and dried flowers into end piece opening, allowing them to rest on the glass circle. Insert remaining glass circle inside end piece opening, working it down until it rests on edges of small tube; see Diagram 4. Secure with small beads of glue.

8. From ½"-wide gold trim, cut a piece long enough to fit around end piece. Glue trim around end piece top edge, slightly overlapping glass circle. From ¼"-wide gold trim, cut two pieces long enough to fit around end piece. Glue one piece around bottom edge. Glue remaining piece 1" from glass end. Slide mirrored end of mailing tube into end piece so tube rests on glass circle inside end piece; see Diagram 5.

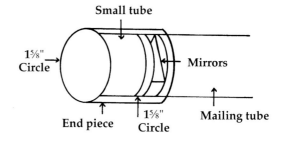

Small tube

1⅝" Circle

Mirrors

End piece   1⅝" Circle   Mailing tube

Diagram 5

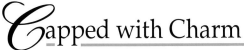

Capped with Charm

These whimsical decorated caps will be holiday gift hits!

MATERIALS (for baseball cap)

Purchased pink baseball cap; matching thread
Hot glue gun and glue sticks
6" piece of 2½"-wide lace trim
One 6"-diameter doily
Needle and thread
¼ yard of ¾"-wide green wired ribbon
2 yards of ½"-wide variegated wired ribbon
1¼ yards of ½"-wide burgundy wired ribbon
One ⅞"-diameter button
One 1⅛"-diameter button
One ½"-diameter rhinestone button
One brass charm

DIRECTIONS

1. Position trim on right-hand side of hat brim, with one edge against base of crown. Hot-glue to brim, gathering slightly for ruffled effect. To make ribbon cascade, glue one edge of green ribbon along base of crown on righthand side, gathering ribbon edge slightly for ruffled effect and covering edge of lace trim. Cut one 7" length from variegated ribbon; knot at 1" intervals. Glue knots along base of crown, repeating ruffled effect.

2. Fold doily in half. Gather bottom loosely to make a fan shape; secure. Glue fan at base of crown on left-hand side of brim, butting one end of ribbons.

3. To make ribbon flower, cut remaining variegated ribbon into thirteen 5" lengths. Tie a loose knot in center of each length. Loop one length so knot is at outer edge. Sew a gathering thread along raw ribbon ends; do not cut thread or remove needle. Repeat with second ribbon length, joining it to first length. Continue joining all ribbon lengths together. Tighten stitches firmly and secure. Shape ribbons into a circle. Wrap thread twice around base of circle and secure; see diagram. Cut burgundy ribbon into ten 4" lengths. Knot and assemble the same as variegated ribbon.

Diagram

4. Glue burgundy ribbon petals inside variegated ribbon petals. Glue completed flower to hat over gathered edge of doily, covering one end of ribbon cascade. Glue rhinestone button to center of flower. Use pink thread to sew through buttonholes so buttons appear to be sewn to cap; brim will be too stiff to sew through. Glue large button to brim over other end of ribbon cascade. Glue remaining button near ribbon flower. Tack or glue charm to ribbon cascade as desired.

MATERIALS (for fisherman's cap)

Purchased white cotton fisherman's cap
   with flip-up brim
Tracing paper
Dressmaker's pen
One hundred ⅛"-diameter glue-on
   red rhinestones
Jewelry glue

DIRECTIONS

1. Trace star pattern opposite. Using dressmaker's pen, transfer pattern to center front of
flip-up brim; see photo. Draw two stars ⅞"
apart on either side of first star.

2. Using jewelry glue, glue one rhinestone to
each dot on star pattern. Allow glue to set.
Wash cap by hand only.

───────────── *Try This* ─────────────

   Trace a scroll pattern, simple floral
design or hearts from wrapping paper or
a greeting card. Transfer to the brim of the
fisherman's cap. Use different-color rhinestones to outline the pattern. Or make a
monogram from rhinestones!

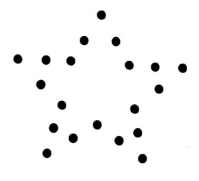

Star Pattern

Opposite: The Biggest Knit Stocking of All

The Biggest Knit Stocking of All

This mountainous stocking can hold a whole sleighful of surprises! (Project pictured on previous page.)

FINISHED SIZE

Approximately 9" wide x 38" long (from top to tip of toe)

MATERIALS

Yarn pictured: Filatura Di Crosa Stella (50 gr., 136-yd. ball): one ball #430 dark red; Filatura Di Crosa Sympathie (50 gr., 146-yd. ball): one ball #734 heather blue, two balls #700 white, one ball #938 dark green; Alpaca Peru (50 gr., 199-yd. ball): one ball #60 brown.

TOOLS AND EQUIPMENT

One pair size 5 knitting needles or size to
    obtain gauge
Four size 5 double-point needles (10" length)
Size E crochet hook
Twelve yarn bobbins
One large stitch holder
Two regular-size stitch holders
Size 16 tapestry needle

Abbreviations

st(s) = stitch(es)	rem = remaining
k = knit	rnd(s) = round(s)
p = purl	pat = pattern
cont = continue	ea = each
tog = together	reg st holder = regular-size
sl = slip	stitch holder
psso = pass slip	lge st holder = large stitch
stitch over	holder
dpn(s) = double-point	
needle(s)	

DIRECTIONS

Gauge: 5 sts and 7 rows = 1".

With red, cast on 90 sts.
Row 1: P 2 (k 2, p 2) across.
Row 2: K 2 (p 2, k 2) across.
Rows 3–9: Alternate Rows 1 and 2. End with Row 1.
Now begin to work chart on pages 94 and 95 from right side facing.
Rows 1–144: Work in stockinette st following chart. Begin with a k row and read chart from right to left. (P rows read left to right.) Increase 1 st at end of row 144—91 sts. End with p row on wrong side.

Checkerboard Pattern: Cont to work in stockinette st using bobbins to change colors. (When changing yarn colors, always twist the new color around the yarn color just ended to prevent holes.)
Rows 1–12: Work 5 sts with red, 9 sts with white, (9 sts red, 9 sts white) 4 times; end with 5 sts red. Fasten off ea bobbin of yarn.

Instep: Row 13 (right side): Sl 23 sts to reg st holder, join red k 9 over previous 9 white sts (join white k 9 sts, join red k 9 sts) 2 times, sl rem 23 sts to a reg st holder.
Rows 14–24: Cont in stockinette st working 9 sts with red, (9 sts white, 9 sts red) 2 times.
Rows 25–36: Work 9 sts with white, (9 sts red, 9 sts white) 2 times. At end of Row 36, place these 45 sts on the lge st holder.

Heel: Sl 23 sts from both reg st holders onto a dpn. With green yarn and right side facing, k across 22 sts, k 2 tog, k 22–45 sts total.

Turning the Heel: Row 1: P 25, p 2 tog, p 1, turn. (This is near center of heel and will decrease 1 st at end of ea row as well as pick up 1 new st from sts on hold on dpn.)
Row 2: Sl 1, [k 5], sl 1, k 1, psso, k 1, turn.
Row 3: Sl 1, [p 6], p 2 tog, p 1, turn.
Row 4: Sl 1, [k 7], sl 1, k 1, psso, k 1, turn.
Row 5: Sl 1, [p 8], p 2 tog, p 1, turn.
Cont in same manner, decreasing one st at end of ea row and adding one more st between [ ] until all sts have been worked—24 sts; fasten off yarn.

Heel Gusset: With green and right side facing, pick up and k 21 sts along side of heel, k across 24 sts on the dpn, pick up and k 21 sts along other side of heel—66 sts.
Row 1: P across.
Row 2: K 1, sl 1, k 1, psso, k to last 3 sts, k 2 tog, k 1.
Repeat these two rows until 44 sts rem. End with a Row 1. Fasten off green yarn.

Foot: Divide 44 sts in half; sl 22 sts to another dpn, leave rem 22 sts on the first dpn. The dividing point is center of heel. Sl the 45 instep sts to third dpn. Beginning at center of heel, work checkerboard pat as follows: With white, increase in first st, k next 3 sts with white, (k 9 sts with red, k 9 sts with white) 4 times, k 9 sts with red; with white, k 2, increase in next st, k 1, join. Cont in stockinette st, work in checkerboard pat for 36 rnds. Fasten off red and white yarn.

Toe: Rnd 1: Join green yarn and work across first dpn: k 20, k 2 tog, k 1; work across second dpn: k 1, sl 1, k 1, psso, k to last 3 sts, k 2 tog, k 1; work across third dpn: k 1, sl 1, k 1, psso, k to last st, k last st and first st of first dpn tog.
Rnd 2: K around.
Repeat Rnds 1 and 2 of toe until 4 sts rem on first dpn, 9 sts rem on second dpn and 5 sts rem on third dpn. K with third dpn across 4 sts on first dpn (sts are now on two dpns). Fasten off, leaving a long yarn tail. Using yarn tail, weave toe sts together with Kitchener stitch; see Diagram. Weave in yarn tails. Sew seam in foot and up back of stocking.

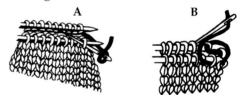

A   B

Diagram

Hanger: Using crochet hook and two strands of red yarn, chain 15, sl st in first chain to form loop. Sew loop to top of stocking on heel side.

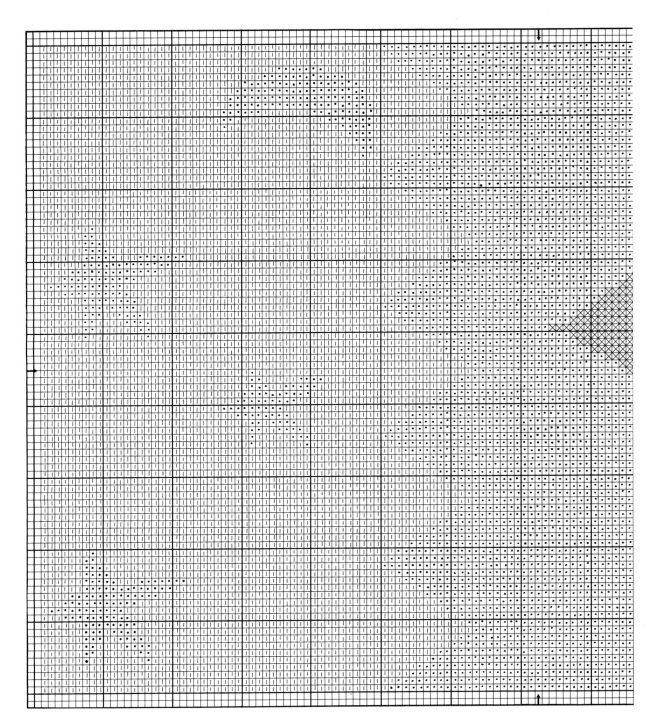

The Biggest Knit Stocking of All Graph
Directions on page 92

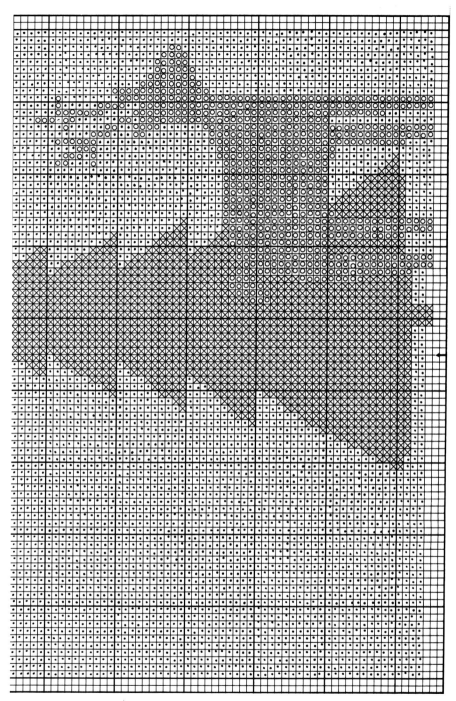

•			Cream
−			Blue
✕			Green
○			Brown

The Biggest Knit Stocking of All Graph
Directions on page 92

ℬeribboned Pinecone Ornament

A few easy steps transform your collection of pretty pinecones into unique and elegant ornaments for tree, mantel or table centerpiece.

MATERIALS (for one)

One medium-size pinecone
¾ yard of each color of ½"-wide wired
   ribbon: pink, burgundy, peach
¾ yard of ½"-wide green wired ribbon
¾ yard of ½"-wide metallic gold wired ribbon
¾ yard of 1½"-wide green velvet ribbon
1 yard of 1⁄16"-wide metallic cord
¼yard of ⅛"-wide metallic cord
6½" of each color of ⅛"-wide grosgrain ribbon:
   green, gold, burgundy
Dressmaker's pen
One small, fancy button
Hot glue gun and glue sticks

DIRECTIONS

1. Cut pink wired ribbon into three 9" lengths. Using dressmaker's pen, mark ½" allowance at each end. Mark off scallops for petals, making each petal about 1⅝" wide; see Diagram 1. Sew a gathering thread along scalloped lines. Tighten thread. Form ribbon into a circle by sewing short ends together. Wrap thread

Stitch along scalloped lines

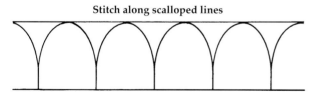

Diagram 1

around stitched end of ribbon circle; secure. Trim excess ribbon below wrapped thread. Fluff ribbon. Repeat with burgundy and peach ribbons, making three flowers each for a total of nine flowers.

2. To make green leaves, cut green wired ribbon into nine 3" lengths. Fold each length into thirds, forming a peak at top end; see Diagram 2. Sew gathering thread through bottom end; pull tight and secure. Cut metallic gold wired ribbon into eight 3" lengths and repeat remainder of Step 2.

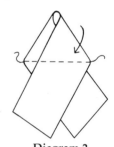

Diagram 2

3. Using dressmaker's pen, make marks at 4" intervals in center of green velvet ribbon, leaving ¾" tail on one end. Sew a small tuck at each mark so ribbon will pucker slightly when formed into loops. Form into five loops and secure with thread. Make a diagonal cut across end of long tail.

4. Glue base of looped velvet ribbon to top of pinecone. Double the ⅛"-diameter metallic cord and knot ends. Glue snugly against velvet ribbon.

5. To make streamers, knot one end of each color of grosgrain ribbon. Glue snugly against velvet ribbon.

6. Gather ⅛"-wide metallic cord into five loose loops, securing each loop with thread. Glue ends to base of velvet ribbon.

7. Glue flowers and leaves to top of pinecone as desired, covering raw edges of velvet ribbon, streamers and metallic cords.

8. Glue fancy button to center of one flower.

Try This

Use smaller pinecones to create unusual and beautiful package ornaments. Tie extra ribbon around the wrapped package, then tie the completed ornament to the front.

Opposite: Holiday Tic-Tac-Toe Game

Holiday Tic-Tac-Toe Game

Create a seasonal version of an old-fashioned game! (Project pictured on previous page.)

MATERIALS

One 7¼" x 7¼" piece of ¾"-thick wood
Medium-grit sandpaper
One 8" x 10" sheet of Mylar
One 12" x 12" piece of mat board
Masking tape
Craft knife
Pencil
Acrylic paints: red, white
Small sponge brush
Colored Sculpey clay: red, white, green
Wax paper
Rolling pin
Paring knife
Hot glue gun and glue sticks

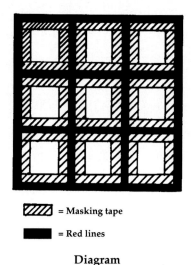

▨ = Masking tape

■ = Red lines

Diagram

DIRECTIONS

1. Lightly sand rough edges of wood until smooth. Trace game board stencil pattern on pages 102 and 103; see "General Instructions" on page 126. Trace tree pattern on page 101. Transfer both patterns onto Mylar. Tape Mylar to mat board. Using craft knife, cut out game board stencil according to pattern. Cut out tree; set aside.

2. Paint top surface of wood with two coats of white, allowing first coat to dry before appying second coat.

3. Place game board stencil on painted surface of wood, aligning edges with edges of wood;

tape in place. Lightly draw in squares with pencil. Remove stencil. Firmly bur-nish masking tape down along edges of squares, which will remain white; see diagram. Use craft knife to make sharp corners with tape, being careful not to score wood.

4. Using sponge brush, paint untaped lines with two coats of red, allowing first coat to dry before applying second coat; see diagram. Also paint edges and bottom of wood with two coats of red. Allow to dry. Carefully remove masking tape. Touch up white squares if needed; allow to dry.

5. To make tree-shaped game pieces, knead green clay in hands until warm and pliable. Place between two sheets of wax paper. Using rolling pin, roll clay to thickness of ⅛". Remove top sheet of wax paper. Place Mylar tree pattern on clay. Using paring knife, cut out five trees; set aside.

6. To make candy cane game pieces, knead red clay in hands until warm and pliable. Roll between palms into ⅛"-diameter tube 28" long. Place on sheet of wax paper. Repeat with white clay. Place red clay tube and white clay tube side by side, matching ends. Cut tubes into ten 2¾" lengths each. Gently coil red and white clay lengths together to form candy cane stripes. Make ten candy canes. Bend hook in one end of each.

7. Bake clay game pieces according to manufacturer's instructions. Cross two candy canes. Glue together where they cross; see photo. Repeat with remaining candy canes.

Try This

Placing the clay in the microwave for 5–10 seconds on medium power makes it ready to work with no kneading!

Clay Tree Pattern

Holiday Tic-Tac-Toe Game
Directions on page 100

One-Half of Game Board
Stencil Pattern

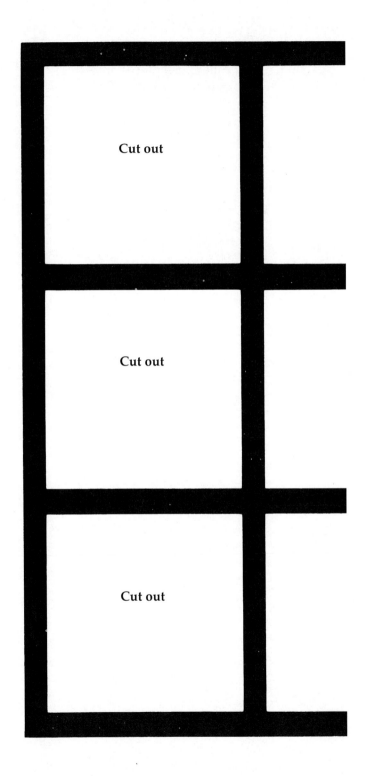

Cut out

Cut out

Cut out

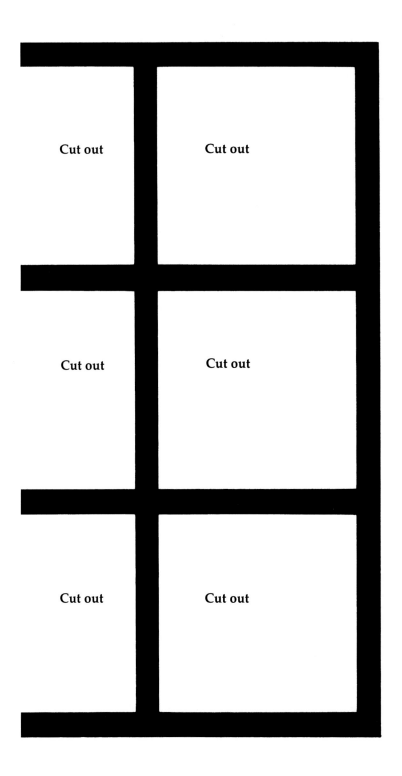

Holiday Tic-Tac-Toe Game
Directions on page 100

One-Half of Game Board
Stencil Pattern

Radish Garden Quilt

Spicy, crunchy radishes adorn a miniature quilt that's perfect for decorating a kitchen or breakfast nook.

FINISHED SIZE

16" wide x 29½" long

MATERIALS

⅜ yard of olive wide-wale corduroy
Scraps of dark green fabric
Scraps of green fabric
⅛ yard of green/cream-striped fabric
Scraps of burgundy fabric
¼ yard of dark red fabric
1¼ yards of rose fabric
¼ yard of mauve print fabric
Scraps of white/mauve print fabric

One 7" x 9" piece of muslin
One ¾" x 4¾" piece of pink/white-striped fabric
½ yard of fleece
Tracing paper
Dressmaker's pen
Thread: dark green, dark red, white
DMC #895 forest green embroidery floss
Embroidery needle
Five ¼"-wide pink buttons

DIRECTIONS

1. Trace radish templates on pages 107, 108 and 109. From corduroy, cut two 7" x 9" pieces, one on the bias. From dark green fabric, cut one each of Templates A, B, C, D, E, F and G. From green fabric, cut one each of Templates H and I and one 2½" x 2½" piece. From green/cream-striped fabric, cut six 1¾" x 7" sashing strips and four 1¾" x 9" sashing

strips. From burgundy fabric, cut one each of Templates J, K and L. From dark red fabric, cut one 7" x 9" piece, one 4¾" x 4¾" piece and one each of Templates M, N and P. From rose fabric, cut one 32" x 19" backing piece (see Step 12) and 1¼"-wide bias strips pieced to make 3 yards of quilt binding. From mauve print fabric, cut eight of Template Q. From fleece, cut one 32" x 19" piece (see Step 12).

2. To prepare left block, transfer entire large radish template to wrong side of bias-cut corduroy piece, centering template in block. Appliqué pieces A through N in place according to template.

3. Center block is a reverse appliqué; see Center Block Diagram on page 106. To complete, mark vertical line on muslin piece 5¾" from and parallel to left long edge. Mark horizontal line 2¾" below and parallel to top short edge. Transfer small radish (Template O) without top to muslin, placing bottom of first radish where vertical and horizontal lines intersect. Place bottom of second radish 2" to the left of first radish bottom, along same horizontal line. Draw a horizontal line 2⅝" below first horizontal line. Place third radish directly below first radish, with bottom on horizontal line. Place next two radishes to the left, ⅝" apart, with bottoms on horizontal line. For last row of radishes, draw a horizontal line 2¾" from and parallel to opposite short edge of muslin. Place last row of radishes upside down and ⅝" apart, with bottoms on horizontal line.

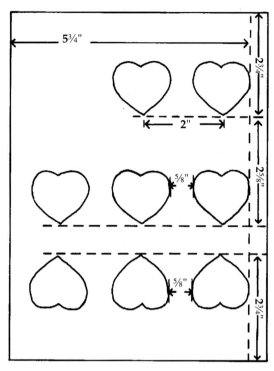

Center Block Diagram

4. Cut out muslin ⅛" inside each radish outline. Place muslin over dark red 7" x 9" fabric piece, aligning edges; baste. Fold under edges of muslin openings to original outlines; slipstitch edges with white thread.

5. Transfer radish top (Template O) to appropriate position above each radish. Using two strands of DMC #895, satin-stitch radish tops. Using white thread, decorate radishes with running stitch; see Template O. Mark three short, curved lines at bottom of each radish for roots; see photo. Sew along lines with running stitch, using red thread.

6. To appliqué right block, fold edges of dark red 4¾" x 4¾" fabric under ¼". Topstitch to wrong side of remaining corduroy piece, 2¾" below and parallel to one short edge and centered horizontally. Fold edges of green 2½" x 2½" piece under ¼". Center on dark red piece and appliqué in place.

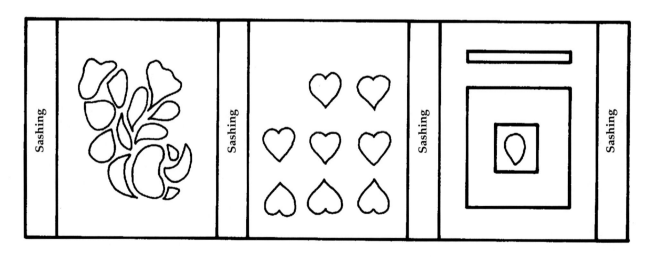

Diagram 1

7. Mark lines around green piece ¼" from and parallel to edges. Fold under edges of Template P and appliqué to center of green piece. Decorate radish with running stitch in white thread. Transfer radish top (Template P) to appropriate place above appliqué. Fill in with running stitch, using white thread.

8. Fold edges of pink strip under ¼". Appliqué to corduroy piece 1" above dark red piece, with long sides parallel to top side of dark red piece. Sew pink buttons to pink strip, centering first button and placing remaining buttons ½" apart on either side.

9. For side sashings, sew one green/cream-striped sashing strip to right and left edges of center block with right sides facing. With right sides facing, sew right block to sashing edge of center block. With right sides facing, sew one sashing strip to right edge of right block. Repeat with left block; see Diagram 1. For top and bottom sashings, sew Template Qs to remaining sashing ends; see Diagram 2. Sew top and bottom sashings to pieced center.

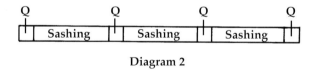

Diagram 2

10. With right sides facing, sew 27" x 3" mauve print border strips to top and bottom edges of pieced center. With right sides facing, sew 17½" x 3" mauve print border strips to sides of pieced center.

11. Layer rose backing piece wrong side up, fleece and quilt top right side up; baste hori-zontally, vertically and diagonally through all. To complete quilt top, quilt in the ditch around pieced center, along green/cream-striped sashing strips and around Template Qs, using red thread. Also using red thread, quilt around radish and top in left block, radishes and tops in center block, radish and top in right block, pink strip and along green stripes in sashing. Using green thread, quilt along marked lines around green square in right block. Using red thread, quilt border strips by following seashell quilting pattern on page 109. Start at right side of each border strip at the seam, rotating quilt while sewing so that each border strip is quilted horizontally.

12. Trim backing and fleece to match quilt top. With right sides facing, sew rose binding to quilt top. Fold binding double to quilt back. Slipstitch binding to quilt back, mitering corners; see "General Instructions" on page 126. Remove basting.

Template Q

Radish Garden Quilt
Directions on page 105

Add ¼" seam allowance to all templates

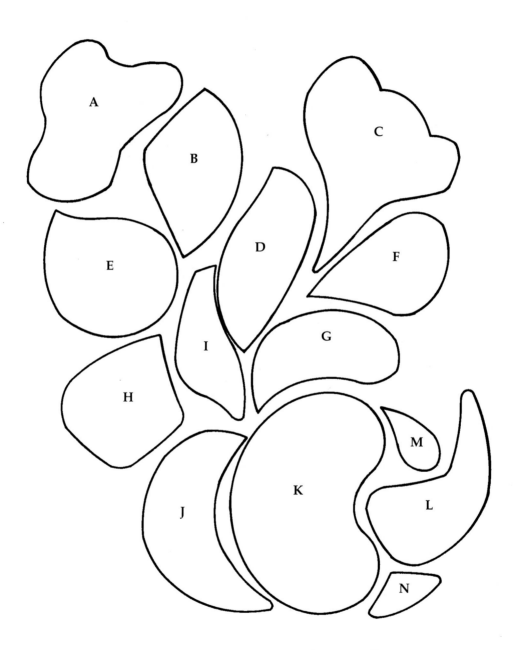

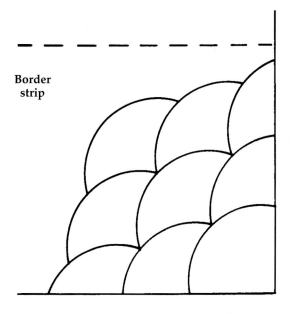

Actual-Size Seashell Quilting Pattern

Border
strip

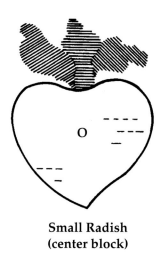

O

**Small Radish
(center block)**

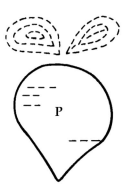

P

**Small Radish
(right block)**

Radish Garden Quilt
Directions on page 105

Add ¼" seam allowance to all templates

*W*inter Wonder Postcard Box

Here's a perfect use for some of those beautiful postcards you've picked up here and there: Create a clever crocheted box.

MATERIALS

Six 6" x 3¾" postcards
One ⅝"-diameter bead

Thread pictured: Schewe Fil D'Ecosse size no.16 (50 gr., 100-m. ball), two balls #163 medium blue.

TOOLS AND EQUIPMENT

Size 7 steel crochet hook
Size 18 tapestry needle
¹⁄₁₆"-diameter paper punch

Abbreviations
ch = chain   sc = single crochet
st(s) = stitch(es)   sl = slip
beg = beginning   ea = each
rnd(s) = round(s)

DIRECTIONS

1. Spacing holes ⅛" apart, punch eighteen holes ⅛" from and parallel to long edges of four postcards, beginning in corners. Spacing holes as before, punch ten holes ⅛" from and parallel to short edges of same cards. (Short edges will have twelve holes, counting corner holes already punched.)

2. Cut remaining two postcards to 3¾" x 3¾" each, centering design as desired. On each, space holes ⅛" apart and punch twelve holes ⅛" from and parallel to two edges, beginning in corners. On each, spacing holes as before, punch ten holes ⅛" from and parallel to remaining two edges. (All edges will have twelve holes, counting corner holes each way.)

3. Bottom and Four Sides (Three 6" x 3¾" and two 3¾" x 3¾" postcards): Using two strands of thread, work around ea postcard section. Beginning in bottom corner hole, work 3 sc, work 3 sc in ea hole around, work 6 sc in ea corner hole, end with 3 sc in beg corner hole; sl st to beg sc. Leave a long tail of yarn for assembly and fasten off.

4. Lid (6" x 3¾" postcard): **Rnd 1:** Beginning at a top corner of edge that will be joined to box, work same as for bottom and sides; do not fasten off, ch 1.
Rnd 2: Work sc in ea sc around; join with sl st to beg ch-1. Fasten off, leaving a long tail for sewing.

5. Assembly: Make sure right sides of postcards are facing outward during assembly. Whipstitch four sides of box together, working through both top loops of each sc. Whipstitch bottom to sides. Whipstitch lid to top of box along previously selected joining edge only. Tack bead to lid at center of front edge.

Crocheted Poinsettias

The poinsettia is the traditional Christmas flower. These lovely crocheted ones will last forever.

FINISHED SIZE

Approximately 12½" diameter. Yarn requirements are for doily and three coasters.

MATERIALS

Yarn pictured: DMC Cébélia size no. 10 (50 gr., 260-m. ball), one ball #699 green; Schewe Fil D'Ecosse size no. 16 (50 gr., 400-m. ball), one ball #157 pale yellow; J. P. Coats Knit-Cro-Sheen (150-yd. ball), two balls #126 Spanish Red; Balger blending filament (50-m. ball), #091 Star Yellow.

TOOLS AND EQUIPMENT

Size 6 steel crochet hook or size to obtain gauge
Size 18 tapestry needle

Abbreviations

ch = chain	sc = single crochet
dc = double crochet	tr = triple
st(s) = stitch(es)	sl = slip
beg = beginning	sp(s) = space(es)
rep = repeat	sk = skip
prev = previous	cl = cluster
lp(s) = loop(s)	ea = each
bet = between	yo = yarn over
bk = back	foll(s) = follow(s)
rnd(s) = round(s)	

DIRECTIONS

Gauge: Approximately 10 sc and 9 rows sc = 1".

Doily flower center: With red, ch 4, join with sl st to form a ring.
Rnd 1: Ch 6, (dc, ch 3 in ring) 7 times, sl st in 3rd ch of beg ch-6—8 sps.
Rnd 2: Sl st into next sp, ch 1, 2 sc in same sp, (ch 3, sc in 3rd ch from hook for picot), 2 sc in same sp, * 2 sc in next sp, (ch 3, sc in 3rd ch from hook for picot), 2 sc in same sp, rep from * 6 times more, end with sl st in beg sc.
First petal: Row 1: Sl in next sc and in picot, ch 12, sk next picot, sl st in next picot, turn.
Row 2: Ch 1, (7 sc, ch 1, 7 sc) in ch-loop, turn.
Row 3: Ch 1, sk next st, sc in bk lp only of ea of next 6 sts, (sc, ch 1, sc) in center ch-1 sp, sc in bk lp only in ea of next 5 sts, sk next st, sc in sc, turn.
Row 4: (Continue to work in bk lp only throughout petal), ch 1, sc in same st, sk next st, sc in ea of next 5 sts, (sc, ch 1, sc) in center ch-1 sp, sc in ea of next 5 sts, sk next st, sc in next sc, turn.
Row 5: Ch 1, sc in same st, sc in ea of next 6 sts, (sc, ch 1, sc) in center ch-1 sp, sc in ea of next 7 sts, turn.
Row 6: Ch 1, sc in same st, sk next st, sc in ea of next 6 sts, (sc, ch 1, sc) in center ch-1 sp, sc in ea of next 6 sts, sk next st, sc in next sc, turn.
Row 7: Ch 1, sc in same st, sc in ea of next 7 sts, (sc, ch 1, sc) in center ch-1 sp, sc in ea of next 8 sts, turn.
Row 8: Ch 1, sc in same st, sk next st, sc in ea of next 7 sts, (sc, ch 1, sc) in center ch-1 sp, sc in ea of next 7 sts, sk next st, sc in next sc, turn.
Row 9: Ch 1, sc in same st, sc in ea of next 8

sts, (sc, ch 1, sc) in center ch-1 sp, sc in ea of next 9 sts, turn.

Row 10: Ch 1, sc in same st, sk next st, sc in ea of next 8 sts, (sc, ch 1, sc) in center ch-1 sp, sc in ea of next 8 sts, sk next st, sc in next sc, turn.

Row 11: Ch 1, sc in same st, sc in ea of next 9 sts (sc, ch 1, sc) in center ch-1 sp, sc in ea of next 10 sts, turn.

Row 12: Ch 1, sc in same st, sk next st, sc in ea of next 9 sts, (sc, ch 1, sc) in center ch-1 sp, sc in next 9 sts, sk next st, sc in next sc, turn.

Row 13: Ch 1, sc in same st, sc in ea of next 10 sts, (sc, ch 1, sc) in center ch-1 sp, sc in ea of next 11 sts, turn.

Row 14: Ch 1, sc in same st, sk next st, sc in ea of next 10 sts, (sc, ch 1, sc) in center ch-1 sp, sc in ea of next 10 sts, sk next st, sc in next sc, turn.

Row 15: Ch 1, sc in same st, sc in ea of next 11 sts, (sc, ch 1, sc) in center ch-1 sp, sc in ea of next 12 sts, turn.

Row 16: Ch 1, sc in same st, sk next st, sc in ea of next 11 sts, (sc, ch 1, sc) in center ch-1 sp, sc in ea of next 11 sts, sk next st, sc in next sc, turn.

Row 17: Ch 1, sc in same st, sc in ea of next 12 sts, (sc, ch 1, sc) in center ch-1 sp, sc in ea of next 13 sts. Fasten off.

Petals 2–4: Row 1: With right sides facing, join red with sl st in same (second) picot as prev petal, ch 12, sk next picot, sl st in next picot, turn.

Rows 2–17: Work same as for first petal.

First leaf: Row 1: With wrong sides facing, join green with sl st in last st of any petal, ch 12, sl st in first st of next petal, turn.

Rows 2–5: Rep Rows 2–5 of first petal. Fasten off.

Leaves 2–4: Row 1: With wrong sides facing, join green with sl st in last st of next petal, ch 12, sl st in first st of next petal.

Rows 2–5: Rep Rows 2–5 of first leaf; do not fasten off after 4th leaf has been worked.

Border: Rnd 1: With right sides facing, ch 4, tr in last leaf st just made, sk 4 sts of next red flower petal (including st where leaf is joined); holding back last lp of ea tr, 2 tr in next st, yo and through rem 3 lps—2-tr cl made, * ch 10, sc in center ch-1 sp of same petal, ch 10, sk next 9 sts of petal, 2-tr cl in next st, sk across to first st of last row of next leaf, work 2-tr cl in first st, ch 10, sc in center ch-1 sp of same leaf, ch 10 **, work 2-tr cl in last st of last row worked of same leaf, work 2-tr cl in 5th st of next petal, rep from * 3 times more, end last rep at **, sl st in top of beg ch-4.

Rnd 2: Ch 1, * 15 sc in next sp, sc in next sc, 15 sc in next sp, sc bet next 2-tr cl, rep from * 7 times more, end with sl st in beg ch-1.

Rnd 3: Ch 4, sk next st, (dc in next st, ch 1, sk next st) around, end with sl st in 3rd ch of beg ch-4.

Rnd 4: Sl st backward into prev ch-1 sp, ch 3, dc in next sp, ch 1, work 2-dc cl as folls: * holding back last lp of ea dc, dc in same sp, dc in next sp, yo and through 3 rem lps on hook—2-dc cl made, ch 1, rep from * around, end with sl st in top of beg ch-3.

Rnd 5: Sl st backward into prev ch-1 sp, ch 3, dc in next ch-1 sp, ch 1, * 2-dc cl working one leg in same sp, and one leg in next sp, ch 1, rep from * around, sl st in top of beg ch-3.

Rnd 6: Rep Rnd 5.

Rnd 7: Ch 4, sc in next sp, [* (sc in next sp, ch 3, sc in same sp—scallop made, rep from * 5 times more, sc in next sp, ch 15, turn, sl st in 4th scallop from ch, ch 3, turn, 25 dc in lp just made, sc in same sp as sc before ch 15, ch 4, turn, sk next dc, dc in next st, ** ch 1, sk next dc, dc in next dc, rep from ** 11 times more, sc in next scallop of Rnd 6, ch 1, turn, (scallop in next sp) 13 times, sc in next ch-1 sp of Rnd 6]—large scallop made, rep bet [ ] until 14 scallops are made (except rep from * 6 times more instead of 5 times more at beg of large scallop), sl st in first ch of beg ch-4 of Rnd 7. Fasten off.

Overlay flower center: With 2 strands of filament and one strand of yellow thread, ch 4, sl st in beg ch to form a ring.
Rnd 1: Ch 6, (dc, ch 3, in ring) 7 times, sl st in 3rd ch of beg ch-6 = 8 sps.
Rnd 2: Ch 1, (sc, ch 6, sc, ch 6, sc, in next sp) 8 times, sl st in beg ch-1 = 16 lps.
Rnd 3: Push lps of Rnd 2 forward, (working through center of next lp of Rnd 2 and into next sp of Rnd 1: sc, ch-3 picot, working through next lp of Rnd 2, sc in same sp of Rnd 1) 14 times, sl st in beg sc of this rnd. Fasten off. With red, sl st in point of any picot and work same as petals in Rows 1–4 of flower.
Assembly: Place overlay on top of flower with points of petals of overlay at points of leaves, tack centers of flowers together, then tack petals to leaves working through the 12th row of petal and the 2nd row of leaves.

Coaster flower center: With yellow thread, work same as for doily.
First petal: Row 1: With right sides facing, join red with sl st in any picot, ch 12, sk next picot, sl st in next picot, turn.
Rows 2–17: Work same as for doily petal.
Petals 2–4: Work same as for doily petals Rows 2–4.
Leaves: With red, work same as Rows 1–4 of doily leaf. Fasten off.

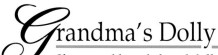

Grandma's Dolly

She resembles a beloved doll that Grandma cherished, but you can lovingly re-create her using pretty fabrics available today.

MATERIALS

8½"-diameter hollow rubber doll head with at least ½"-diameter neck opening
8" of ⅜"-diameter dowel
Drill with ⅛" bit
#10 x 1"-long screw
Premixed papier-mâché
Newspapers
Shallow pan
Acrylic paints: cranberry, pink, blue, brown, black, tan, green, cream
Paintbrushes
2½ yards of ¼"-wide cording
Hot glue gun and glue sticks
Tracing paper
Dressmaker's pen
5"-long dollmaker's needle
Plastic beans
1 yard of ¾"-wide cording
¼ yard of muslin; matching thread
½ yard of tan fabric; white thread
Scrap of green

print fabric
Four 4"-diameter fabric doilies
¼ yard of green/black print fabric; matching thread
¼ yard of red-checked fabric; matching thread
⅛ yard of burgundy print fabric
Scrap of green/white print fabric
¼ yard of green-on-green print fabric
1½ yards of 1½"-wired red ribbon
⅝ yard of 1/16"-wide metallic gold/orange ribbon
½ yard of 1/16"-wide metallic gold/blue ribbon
Sprig of plastic holly with wire stem
Twelve small silk flowers with wire stems
Three silk leaves with wire stems
9" length of florist's wire
2"-wide costume jewelry brooch

DIRECTIONS

All seams are ¼".

1. Drill a hole 3" from one end of dowel; insert opposite end of dowel into dolly head through neck. To hold dowel in place, insert screw through top of dolly head into dowel; see Diagram 1.

2. Cut newspapers into ½"-wide and ¼"-wide strips. Pour premixed papier-mâché in pan. Dip newspaper strips one at a time in papier-mâché and apply a thin layer to dolly head, molding strips to features. Allow to dry. Paint doll head cream. Allow to dry. Paint facial details as follows; eyes green, eyebrows brown, pupils black and lips cranberry. Dilute pink paint with water and lightly paint cheeks; see photo. Allow to dry.

3. To make hair, cut and shape ¼" cording in curls, spirals, zigzags or straight lengths, gluing to head. Paint hair tan. Allow to dry.

4. Enlarge pattern for dolly body on page 120, transferring all information; see "General Instructions" on page 126. Trace gusset and hand patterns on pages 120 and shoe pattern

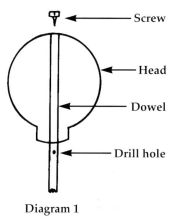

Diagram 1

Labels: Screw, Head, Dowel, Drill hole

117

on page 121, transferring all information. From muslin, cut two body pieces and one gusset. Also from muslin, cut one 2" x 33" strip. From tan fabric, cut four hands; set aside. Also from tan fabric, cut ½"-wide bias strips, piecing as needed to equal 2 yards; set aside. Fromgreen print fabric, cut two shoes; set aside.

5. With right sides facing, fold muslin strip in half lengthwise; sew along long edge to make tube. Turn. Cut tube into two 10½" lengths for legs and two 6" lengths for arms. From ¾" cording, cut two 9½" lengths for legs and two 5" lengths for arms.

6. To make dolly leg, attach safety pin to end of one 9½" length of cording. Draw cording through one 10½" muslin tube, leaving a ½" muslin overhang at each end. Using zipper foot, sew tube ends closed very close to cording ends. Repeat with remaining 10½" muslin tube and 9½" length of cording. To make arm, repeat process with 5" lengths of cording and 6" muslin tubes.

7. Sew legs securely to gusset bottom at seam allowance and between dots. Sew one arm to each side of dolly body front between dots. Wrap arms and legs firmly with tan bias strip, tacking bias to muslin tubes at beginning and end of wrapping. To make hand, machine satin-stitch edges of two hands together, using white thread. Stuff loosely. Repeat with remaining two hands. Slide one hand over end of each arm; slipstitch.

8. With right sides facing, sew gusset to bottom edges of body pieces, securing leg ends in seam. Sew across leg tops very close to cording ends to tack to dolly body front. Sew body pieces together, leaving top of neck open. Sew double gathering thread around

neck; do not cut thread. Stuff body firmly with plastic beans to within 2" of neck opening. Insert dowel into body through neck opening. Fill remainder of body with plastic beans. Tighten gathering thread at neck and secure. Using thread and dollmaker's needle, secure dowel to body through drilled hole.

9. Trace pattern for dolly bodice on page 121. From burgundy print fabric, cut two bodices. For pantaloons, cut two 8" x 6" strips from green-on-green print fabric. For underskirt, cut one 24" x 9" strip from red-checked fabric. For apron, cut one 24" x 6" strip from green/black fabric. For apron border, cut one 24" x 2" strip from green/white fabric.

10. With right sides facing, sew together underarm side seams of two bodices. Turn. Slip bodice over dolly's head and arms. Using double strand of white thread, whipstitch raw edges of shoulder seams together, ending at neck on each side. Turn sleeves up to make cuffs; tack a tuck in end of each sleeve.

11. To make pinafore strap, fold two doilies in half. Tack together at fold, overlapping doilies ½"; see Diagram 2. Place across dolly's shoulder with tacked point at top; see photo. Tack ends to front and back of body. Repeat with remaining two doilies.

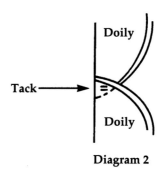

Diagram 2

12. To make pantaloon, sew together long edges of one green print strip with right sides facing. Turn. Slip pantaloon over dolly leg. Make a tuck at top and tack to leg near body. Repeat for other pantaloon.

13. To make underskirt, fold one long edge of red-checked strip under ⅜" and hem, using white thread. With right sides facing, sew together short edges of strip. Turn. Sew gathering thread at long edge; do not cut thread. Slip underskirt onto doll. Tighten gathering threads at waist and secure. Tack underskirt to body.

14. To make apron border, cut ¾"-deep zig-zags in one long edge of green/white strip, using Diagram 3 as a guide. With right sides facing, sew straight edge of border to one long edge of green/black strip. With wrong sides facing, sew together short edges of pieced strip to complete apron. Turn. Sew gathering thread on long edge; do not cut thread. Slip apron onto doll, covering ends of doilies. Tighten gathering threads at waist and secure; tack to body.

15. To make shoe, sew gathering thread on one shoe according to pattern; do not cut

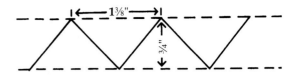

Diagram 3

thread. Hold shoe wrong side up and fold shoe strap to right side. Place shoe behind dolly foot and bring strap ends to front; knot. Fold shoe to front of foot, tucking fabric according to pattern. Tighten gathering threads around foot and secure. Sew shoe front edges to foot. Repeat with remaining shoe and foot.

16. Wrap red ribbon twice around dolly's waist and tie in a bow at the front. Cut metallic gold/orange ribbon in half and tie one piece in a bow around each wrist. Tie metallic gold/blue ribbon in a bow around head. Wrap stem of holly sprig around hair ribbon, securing with glue if needed. Wrap florist's wire around neck. Wrap stems of flowers and leaves around wire as desired; see photo. Pin brooch to bodice front.

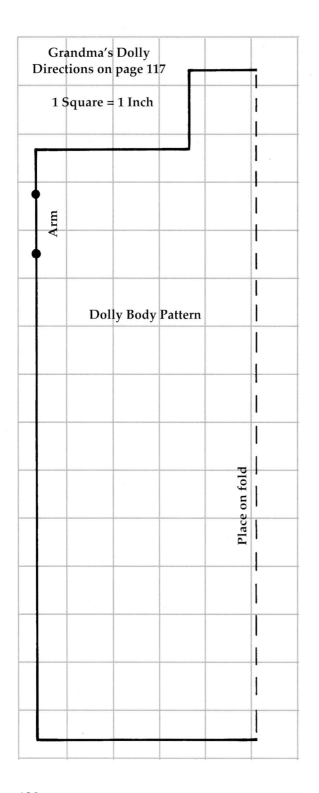

Grandma's Dolly
Directions on page 117

1 Square = 1 Inch

Arm

Dolly Body Pattern

Place on fold

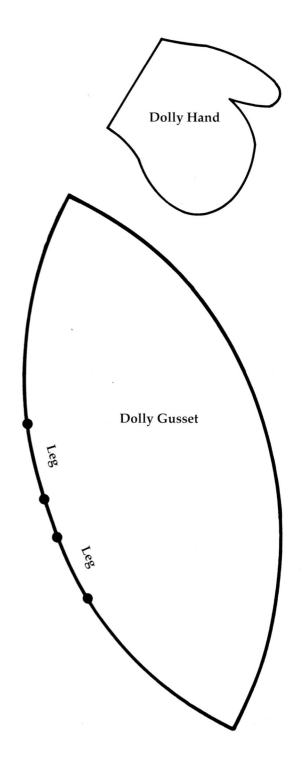

Dolly Hand

Dolly Gusset

Leg

Leg

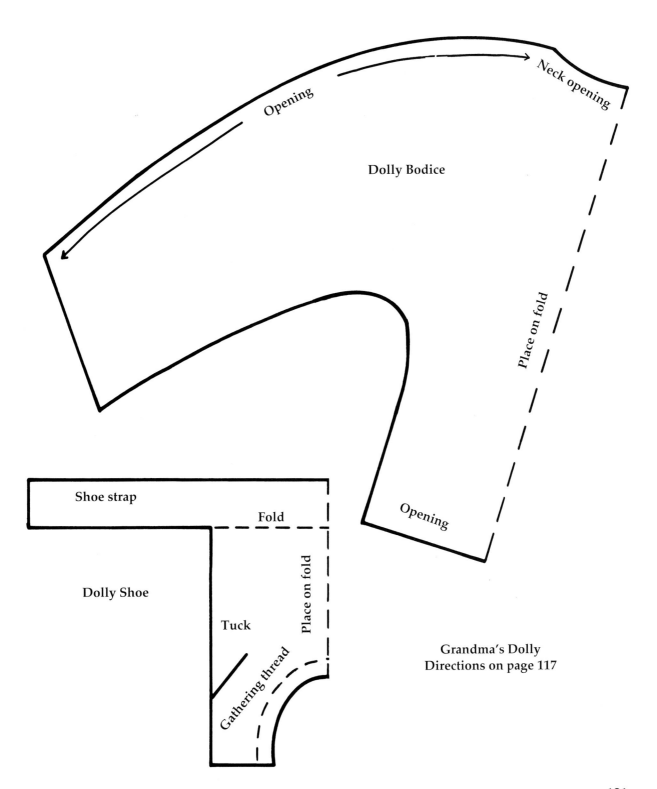

Opening

Neck opening

Dolly Bodice

Place on fold

Opening

Shoe strap

Fold

Dolly Shoe

Tuck

Place on fold

Gathering thread

Grandma's Dolly
Directions on page 117

121

✐tar~Struck Checkerboard

This pieced fabric checkerboard wallhanging, buttoned up and anchored with stars, is a natural for a game room or den.

MATERIALS

⅛ yard of blue/gray-checked fabric; matching thread
Scraps of rust, purple, gray, brown and country blue fabrics
¼ yard of white fabric
Five ⅝"-diameter decorative brown buttons
Four 1"-long white star buttons
One 14" x 14" piece of fleece

DIRECTIONS
All seams are ¼".

1. Trace block patterns A and B on page 124. From rust fabric, cut five As and two Bs. From purple fabric, cut eight As and one B. From gray fabric, cut twelve As. From brown fabric, cut eight As and one B. From blue fabric, cut twelve As. From white fabric, cut four As, two 1¾" x 11" strips and two 1¾" x 14" strips. From checked fabric, cut four 2¼" x 7½" strips.

2. Piece checkerboard center from A blocks; see diagram for color placement. Sew one B to each end of one checked strip; repeat with second checked strip and two Bs. Sew two remaining checked strips to right and left edges of checkerboard center. Sew strips with Bs attached to top and bottom edges of checkerboard center, covering ends of other checked strips. Sew on buttons according to diagram on page 124.

3. Sew one 11" white strip to top edge of hanging. Sew remaining 11" strip to bottom edge. Trim excess if needed. Sew one 14" white strip to each remaining edge of hanging. Trim excess if needed. Baste fleece to wrong side of hanging along edges, trimming excess fleece.

4. Frame hanging as desired.

Star-Struck Checkerboard
Directions on page 123

	R	P	G	C	G	P	R	
☆ P								☆ R
	R	P	G	C	G	P	R	
	P	G	C	•B	C	G	P	
	G	C	B	W	B	C	G	
	C	•B	W	•R	W	•B	C	
	G	C	B	W	B	C	G	
	P	G	C	•B	C	G	P	
	R	P	G	C	G	P	R	
☆ R								B ☆

Color Key

R = Rust	C = Country blue
P = Purple	B = Brown
G = Gray	W = White

• = Button placement
☆ = Star button placement

Diagram

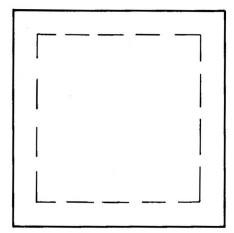

Block Pattern B

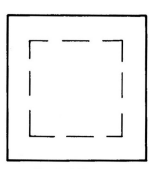

Block Pattern A

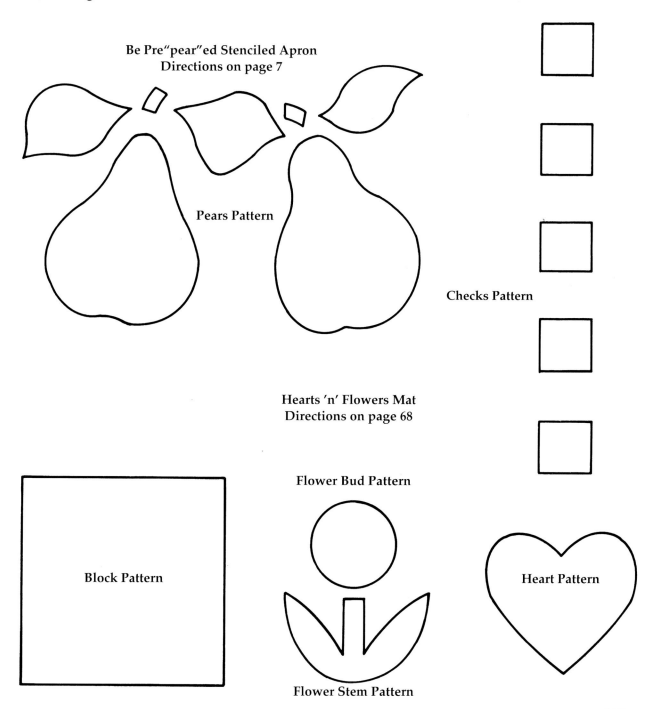

Be Pre"pear"ed Stenciled Apron
Directions on page 7

Pears Pattern

Checks Pattern

Hearts 'n' Flowers Mat
Directions on page 68

Flower Bud Pattern

Block Pattern

Heart Pattern

Flower Stem Pattern

 General Instructions

Easy Reference Features

Materials: The Materials List identifies the items used and the quantity needed to finish the model shown in the photograph.

Directions: The directions offer step-by-step guidance for completing the model shown in the photograph, plus helpful hints.

Transferring Patterns: Use tracing paper or Mylar to trace patterns. Transfer all information. For projects requiring sewing, the patterns include a ¼" seam allowance. Patterns to be transferred to fusible webbing are printed reversed; when fused and turned, they will be correct. Patterns not printed with their project are found on page 125.

Enlarging Patterns: Patterns too large for the page are prepared on a grid in which each square is equal to 1" on the finished pattern. To enlarge a pattern, use paper large enough for the finished pattern size. Mark grid lines 1" apart to fill the paper. Mark dots on these lines corresponding to the pattern. Connect the dots. Fabric stores supply paper with dots preprinted at 1" intervals. You may also use a copy machine or 1" graph paper.

Cross-Stitch Guidelines

The symbols on the graph each represent a different color. Refer to the code to verify which color and stitch to use. The code also indicates the brand of floss used to stitch the model, as well as the cross-reference for using another brand. Use the number of floss strands called for. The symbols on the code match the graph. A symbol under a diagonal line indicates a half cross-stitch; see "Stitches" on the next page.

Sewing Hints

Corded Piping: Piece bias strips together to equal the required length. Place the cording in the center of the wrong side of the bias strip. Fold bias strip over, aligning raw edges. Using a zipper foot, stitch close to the cording through both layers of fabric. Trim the seam allowance to ¼".

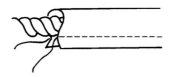

Mitering Corners: Mitering adds a crisp finish to corners on borders and bindings. Mitered borders have diagonal seams in the corner. To miter a corner, sew up to, but not through, the seam allowance; back tack. Repeat on all four edges, making stitching lines meet exactly at corners. Fold two adjacent border pieces together as shown in the diagram. Mark, then sew at a 45-degree angle. Trim the seam allowance to ¼".

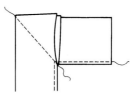

Tassels: Wind fiber around cardboard rectangle as many times as desired; see Diagram A. Secure bundle with strand of fiber; see Diagram B. Cut untied strands; see Diagram C. Tightly wrap a single strand around bundle about one-third of the way down; see Diagram D. Tie ends. Push ends into tassel to hide them. Trim tassel to desired length.

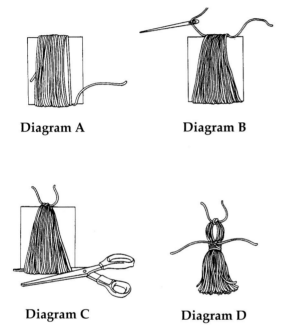

Diagram A   Diagram B

Diagram C   Diagram D

Craft Hints

Working with Glue: Keep a shallow dish of warm water and a clean cloth handy. Dip fingers in water and dry them on cloth to remove glue before handling fabric.

To control overspray when using spray adhesive, protect unglued areas with a scrap of paper and cover work surface with newspapers. Replace sticky newspapers before gluing next item. Keep spray away from hot glue gun or open flame.

When gluing fabric, begin along one edge, smoothing fabric as you apply it to avoid bubbles or wrinkles. When folding excess fabric to back of any item, keep even tension. Trim corners and check fit before gluing in place.

Marking and Cutting Fabric: Tape fabric to work surface before marking. Do not stretch fabric as you tape it; allow it to lie naturally. Remove tape as needed for smooth cutting. If fabric edges begin to ravel, lightly apply antifray liquid.

Stitches

Cross-Stitch and
Half Cross-Stitch

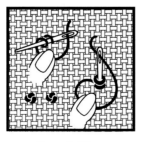

French Knot

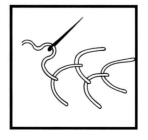

Feather Stitch

Lazy Daisy

uppliers

For a merchant near you, write to one of the suppliers below.

Aida 18
Murano 30
Marlitt thread
Zweigart/Joan Toggitt Ltd.
Weston Canal Plaza, 35 Fairfield Place
West Caldwell, NJ 07006

Acrylic paints
Stencil Magic Paint Cream
Delta Technical Coatings, Inc.
2550 Pellissier Place
Whittier, CA 90601

Balger metallic thread
Kreinik Mfg. Co., Inc.
P.O. Box 1966
Parkersburg, WV 26101

Coaster with glass insert
Sudberry House
Box 895
Old Lyme, CT 06371

DMC floss
DMC Cébélia yarn
The DMC Corporation
Port Kearney, Building #10
South Kearny, NJ 07032

Doll hat
Dainty Details Hatworks
26711 Granvia Drive
Mission Viejo, CA 92691

Filatura Di Crosa yarns
Stacy Charles Collection
117 Dobbins Street
Brooklyn, NY 11222

Glue
Aleene's
A Division of Artis, Inc.
85 Industrial Way
Buellton, CA 93427

J.&P. Coats Knit-Cro-Sheen
Coats & Clark, Inc.
Dept. C01, P.O. Box 1010
Toccoa, GA 30577

Polyester stuffing
Fleece
Fairfield Processing Corporation
88 Rose Hill Avenue
P.O. Drawer 1157
Danbury, CT 06810

Porcelain jars and lids
Anne Brinkley Designs Inc.
21 Ransom Road
Newton Centre, MA 02159

Schewe yarns
Muench Yarns
118 Ricardo Road
Mill Valley, CA 94941

Seed beads
Mill Hill division of
Gay Bowles Sales, Inc.
P.O. Box 1060
Janesville, WI 53547

Sewing machine
Bernina of America
3500 Thayer Court
Aurora, IL 60504-6182